quietreflections
of hope

120 Devotions to Start Your Day

quietreflections
of hope

Revell
a division of Baker Publishing Group
Grand Rapids, Michigan

© 2009 by The Livingstone Corporation

Published by Revell
a division of Baker Publishing Group
P.O. Box 6287, Grand Rapids, MI 49516-6287
www.revellbooks.com

Printed in China

ISBN 978-0-8007-1928-9

Scripture is taken from GOD'S WORD®. Copyright 1995 by God's Word to the
Nations. Used by permission of Baker Publishing Group. All rights reserved.

Produced with the assistance of The Livingstone Corporation (www.
LivingstoneCorp.com). Project staff includes Linda Taylor, Betsy Schmitt, Linda
Washington, Dana Niesluchowski. Cover and interior designs by Larry Taylor
and Lindsay Galvin. Production by Larry Taylor and Lindsay Galvin.

Welcome

When you enter a home or a new environment, what makes you feel most welcome? A hug or a smile meant especially for you? A warm handshake and eyes meeting yours with a look of patent understanding? Consider this: God wants to welcome you into the warmth of His presence every morning—to begin your day sitting at His feet with contentment and expectation. He wants to share your joys and your sorrows and give you strength to face the day ahead.

This devotional includes 120 meditations to facilitate your time with God each morning. Each meditation includes a Scripture passage, an inspirational thought, an ending prayer, and a beautiful color photo to help you reflect on the truths discussed. Consider the prayer a jumping-off point to your own conversation with God.

So come and be like Mary, making what Jesus called "the right choice" (Luke 10:42). Refuse to be distracted by what lies ahead today and instead sit at Jesus' feet and focus on what you really need—a word from Him. He wants to give you quiet reflections of hope to start your day.

You're welcome to stay as long as you like.

—*The Editors*

Contributors

Heather Cox

Jennifer Devlin

Carol Chaffee Fielding

Kathy Hardee

Jennifer A. Haynes

Kathy Lay

Frances L. Lewis

Brenda Nixon

Erin P. O'Connor

Robin Priestley

Sue Rosenfeld

Maggie Wallem Rowe

Hilary S. Sahli

Debbie Simler-Goff

Kathryn A. Spurgeon

Amber E. Susek

Michelle Van Loon

God named the light day, and the darkness he named night.
There was evening, then morning—the first day.
Genesis 1:5

A New Day Dawns

ay and night, night and day—a perpetual cycle instituted on the very first day of creation. Don't you love that God works in cycles? It shows in the changing of seasons, the ebb and flow of tides, and the waxing and waning of the moon. Isn't it comforting to know that bleak winter melts into glorious spring, that the valley floor ascends to the mountaintop, and that darkness is chased away by the light?

Even the very darkest day of all, the Friday of Jesus' death, was resolved in a sublime early morning a few days later. Through pain, persecution, and crucifixion, Jesus knew the outcome all along. That hope, that promise from His Father God, saw Him through His dark night and tinged His proclamation on the cross, "It is finished!" with a resounding note of triumph.

That hope is now your hope. His crown of thorns was traded for a crown of glory . . . so yours will be. His wounded, beaten, and crushed body was restored . . . so yours will be.

His sorrow marked a dark period, but oh, did joy ever come with the morning! And so it will be for you as you cling to that amazing promise that dark is always followed by light for God's children, a hint He wrote across the sky on that very first day. Welcome and bask in the divine light He provides you on this brand new morning.

Father God,

how faithful You are!
Thank You for the
promise that even though
I may weep in a season of
darkness, You'll provide
the light to chase it away.
Guide me to claim that
hope this morning and
every morning to live my
days in and for You.

Dear Lord,

I lay my life before You this morning, burdens and all. Please deliver me in a way that proves You alone are God.

> *Hezekiah took the letters from the messengers, read them, and*
> *went to the LORD's temple. He spread them out in front of the LORD*
> *and prayed to the LORD. "LORD of Armies, God of Israel, you are enthroned*
> *over the angels. . . . Turn your ear toward me, LORD, and listen."*
> *2 Kings 19:14–16*

Letters to God

Do you feel, as Hezekiah did so many years ago, that this is "a day filled with misery, punishment, and disgrace" (2 Kings 19:3)? Life sometimes crashes in, leaving nothing but hopelessness in its wake. Is a broken relationship, poor health, or an unbearable situation crushing your spirit? If so, this morning's Scripture is for you.

Sennacherib, king of Assyria, struck fear in the hearts of the Israelites. His army had captured every city except Jerusalem. Confident that he would also conquer Judah, Sennacherib taunted the Israelites. He hoped to instill in the Israelites a fear of the enemy that was stronger than their faith in God.

Hezekiah took the life-threatening letters of ultimatum delivered by Sennacherib's messengers and spread them out before the Lord in His temple. And he prayed, asking God to turn His ear toward him and listen to his request. Hezekiah knew that without God's intervention, the city of Jerusalem could not hold its own against the mighty Assyrian army. But Hezekiah knew that God's power could trump that of any invading army. Instead of being terrified, King Hezekiah held fast to what he knew to be true about his God.

When troubles arise and your faith begins to falter, your God stands ready to help. Spread out your request before God and pray that He will listen. Remember that His power is mightier than any battle you face today.

Moses called Bezalel and Oholiab and every other
craftsman to whom the LORD *had given these skills*
and who was willing to come and do the work.
Exodus 36:2

God's Refrigerator Art

Your preschool daughter clutches a fat purple crayon in her hand. Her arm is sweeping across the paper as she fills a fresh sheet of white paper with colorful circles. Her joyous effort looks like fireworks on a warm summer night. She offers it to you proudly.

"For me? Thank you!" you respond, giving her a hug. "I have the perfect spot for this." You head to the refrigerator and use a couple of magnets to position her offering so everyone in your home can admire it.

In ancient Israel, two men named Bezalel and Oholiab spent their childhood years faithfully growing in their skills as artisans. By the time they were adults, God called upon them to lead the crew of master craftsmen who would create the interior of the worship center for the nation. However, Bezalel and Oholiab's skills were not the sole reason for their divine job assignment; these men had also distinguished themselves because they'd been faithful to the Lord. (Bezalel, in fact, is the first person named in Scripture said to be filled with the Spirit of God.) Their work was an offering of love, flowing out of their relationship with God.

He welcomes the gifts your unique skills create the same way you celebrate the crayoned artwork of your child. He celebrates your offering and places it in the perfect spot to reflect His glory. Whatever tasks you face today, ask God to show you how you can use your gifts and glorify Him in the process.

❧ Father,

I am grateful for who You are and what You've done for me. I worship You. I want all that I do today to create a beautiful offering to You. Please transform the work of my hands into Your "refrigerator art." May what I do today be beautiful for You.

Creator God,

thank You for Your mercy and
amazing love. Today, as I interact
with family and friends, let
me feel Your presence in my
life and witness Your love for
Your people. Help me to share
the hope I have in You just as
brightly as You beam a rainbow's
colors across the sky. Lead me
to faith-filled adventures and to
a path of obedience as I follow
Your calling on my life.

I will put my rainbow in the clouds to be a
sign of my promise to the earth.
Genesis 9:13

Following the Rainbow

o you remember the first time your eyes caught sight of a
rainbow arching through the afternoon sky? The rain beat
down on the pavement followed by the stripes of God's love gleam-
ing through the newly sunlit atmosphere after the drifting clouds
shifted—truly a wondrous sight! Your childhood imagination was
surely set on finding the treasure at the end of the multicolored trail.

Following the path to the rainbow's end with your eyes may have
been fun as a child, but as a beautiful woman of God, the multihued
exhibit signifies so much more than an appealing display. God created this dramatic miracle as a sign and a promise to all the earth that
we will never again be destroyed in a flood such as in Noah's day.

Noah was not a fairy tale character; he was a follower of God Most
High who obediently built the ark just as the Lord had instructed.
Noah and his small family became faith-filled pioneers of a new
beginning for the earth—and for you and me. That rainbow you have
chased more than once in your life is a promise to you of God's mercy
and love.

His love is unfailing and unceasing. Today, as you start your day,
praise God for His abundant love for you and His mercy toward the
earth.

They were appointed to stand to give thanks and praise to the LORD every morning. They were appointed to do the same thing in the evening.
1 Chronicles 23:30

Salty

Daily the Levites performed many tasks in the temple of God. Ordinary jobs included baking the special bread used in the temple. Special rituals included preparing for the reverential sacrifices on holy days. Two of their daily appointed jobs, thanksgiving and praise, salted everything, flavoring every mundane task and every traditionally rich service. In thanking and praising God every morning and every evening, even the dullest of their routine tasks became worship.

What a recipe of rich spiritual growth for each of us! Suppose you made a daily appointment to praise and thank God each morning, asking that every task of the day become "salted" with worship? The senior citizen in front of you at the supermarket would become an opportunity to serve and not a temptation to become impatient. A whining child might give cause for thanks that she could cry and you could hear. The fantastic miracle of Christ's love that you realize on Sunday would not so easily flee from your heart, crushed by the beatings of Monday's mundane. Each morning appointment with God might cause you to be more cognizant of God's moving because you would know that daily it is your responsibility to find something for which to be grateful.

So rise, meet that daily appointment of praising and thanking the Lord. Enjoy your newly flavored walk with Him more fully!

Father,

help me to choose to have a daily morning appointment to praise and thank You. May my life be salted with worship today so that even the mundane tasks become acts of worship to You.

Lord God,
who do You want to encourage through me today? Show me who I can encourage and how best I can do that.

The Almighty LORD will teach me what to say, so I will know how to encourage weary people. Morning after morning he will wake me to listen like a student.

Isaiah 50:4

A Touch of Encouragement

This verse says that God awakens you "morning after morning," wanting to teach you as a teacher with a student. The context of this passage is the Lord's special servant describing His obedience in contrast to the disobedience of God's people, Israel. Because this servant is willing to learn, God promises to teach. This servant will bring special encouragement to God's weary people.

The passage works for believers as well. God willingly wakes you morning after morning, wanting to teach you. He has a message for a world in sorrow and pain, and the message comes through the hands, feet, and mouths of His followers. The Lord desires that you be His light in the dark world, bringing the kind of encouragement only God can give to people weary of sin and suffering.

So many people need encouragement. Often it can be difficult to even be aware when someone has a need or, if you are aware, to know what to say or how to help. So it makes sense to pay attention in God's classroom this morning. Ask God to show you, as you walk through your day today, who could use a kind word, a soft touch, a big hug, even a simple smile and a thank you. A little encouragement can bring sunshine into someone's dark world.

What can you do to bring encouragement into your world today?

Have you ever given orders to the morning or
assigned a place for the dawn?
Job 38:12

God's System

very book has an assigned place at the library. Each novel, biography, or science fiction has its own call number that tells the librarian where the book should be placed. Each shelf holds specific books in a specific order. Without organization, a library would be total chaos—piles of books strewn across shelves. Without a system, books would become almost unusable for no one could find what they needed. Organization makes all that information easy to find and available.

Imagine the universe without organization—the earth orbiting at whatever speed in whatever orbit, leaving some of us to freeze and others to scorch. Or what if the seasons came and went in whatever order they wanted, whenever they wanted? What if you never knew whether spring, summer, or fall would follow winter—or if winter would end at all? Fortunately, God has a system of organization. He has precisely designated the location of each star and calculated the rotation of each planet. In the midst of this system, He has "assigned a place for the dawn."

If God can keep the universe in order, surely He can help you handle your day. Like an extremely well-organized library, nothing goes amiss with Him in charge. Sip your coffee, watch the sun rise, and let Him take care of the order of your life.

God,

You are so amazing! I cannot comprehend the width and breadth of You. You are so wonderfully organized. Please help me see Your majestic order in my life today.

꧁ *Lord God,*

Orchestrator of the sunrise, I
come to You in the quiet of
this morning. I bring You this
day with all its possibilities,
and ask that You will use it for
Your glory. Please reveal Yourself to me in Your quiet glory,
and help me to be patient as I
wait for Your voice.

*In the morning, O LORD, hear my voice. In the
morning I lay my needs in front of you, and I wait.*
Psalm 5:3

His Quiet Glory

hether hiking, biking, or just sleeping out, surely a great
pleasure of life is to curl up in a sleeping bag under the
stars. If you awake in the early morning before the sun has risen, before your companions are stirring, before coffee and bacon and eggs,
there is a hush over the world. Droplets of dew rest on your sleeping
bag and it seems like the night is still very much around you.

Then slowly, silently, almost imperceptibly, you begin to see a
change in the sky. You can't put your finger on it, but the stars seem
to fade and the inky blackness lightens into a cold gray. Then gradu-
ally the gray takes on warmer hues. None of this happens quickly.
Everything seems to be holding its breath for something. Suddenly,
brilliantly, a bright light highlights the edges of the hills. The sun has
risen, with all of its beauty, promise, and hope.

Whether it is still dark outside or you're reading these words with
the sun already moving up the sky, take these moments to come before God, offering Him your entire day. As you bring Him praise and
lay your needs before Him, take just a few moments to wait. Listen.
Breathe. In those moments, God's Spirit will imperceptibly relax your
heart and feed your soul. You may not be able to pinpoint the moment it happens, but you'll know, when you arise to take on the day,
that God has touched you with His light.

We wait for the LORD. He is our help and our shield. In him our hearts find joy. In his holy name we trust. Let your mercy rest on us, O LORD, since we wait with hope for you.
Psalm 33:20–22

Unexpected Showers

Look down on any city street on a rainy day and you'll see a colorful sea of umbrellas—portable roofs keeping the elements at bay. Yellow, pink, clear, striped, even Impressionist-painting-themed umbrellas jostle against basic black as people make their way through the rain to their next destination. A few people, here and there, got caught without an umbrella and so use a purse or newspaper as they scamper as fast as they can to avoid the raindrops. Most everyone (except for the occasional free spirit) looks to shield hair and clothing from the rain.

When trials and difficulties pour down all around you and it seems like troubles rain from the dark sky, God says that He is your help and shield. Like an umbrella, He covers and protects you from the worst of the storm. Whatever drips into your life today, your Lord is there to help keep you warm, safe, and dry. You don't have to worry or fret because He is protecting you.

As you venture out today—whether the sky is sunny or whether dark clouds threaten—don't forget your "umbrella." In that, your heart can find joy. In Him, you can trust. His mercy will rest on you because you wait with hope for Him.

Dear Lord,

please be my shield for the day. Protect me and help me see joy through the difficulties that may arise.

Thank You, Father,

for walking beside me through life and being willing to carry my burdens. Please help me to remember to give them to You each day so I can be free.

*Thanks be to the Lord, who daily carries our
burdens for us. God is our salvation.*
Psalm 68:19

Your Backpack

The elementary school starts at nine o'clock in the morning. Groups of children make their way along the neighborhood sidewalks. Occasionally a mom walks alongside a very young child, providing safety and security from the doorway at home to the school entrance. Sometimes the child's backpack just gets too heavy for the walk and he passes it off to his mom—whose shoulders are much bigger and stronger. As they walk to school together, mom carries the burden and the little boy skips along beside her.

A child's backpack holds the necessities of the day—schoolbooks, pencils, paper, bag lunch—but even so, sometimes it's just too heavy for his little shoulders. What are you carrying with you today? What's in your "backpack"? Worries about money, discontent in a difficult relationship, or maybe concern for an elderly relative? Perhaps you carry sadness, grief, or anger. Sometimes strong emotions can become extremely heavy, but any burden—whether great or small—can impede your freedom to be the person God wants you to be.

When your burden gets too heavy, remember that your heavenly Father walks on the sidewalk of life beside you, always willing and anxious to carry your heavy load. So get rid of that backpack! Hand it over! And once you pass your burden on to Him, you will be free to skip along beside Him, and maybe even do a few cartwheels!

> *I look up toward the mountains. Where can*
> *I find help? My help comes from the LORD,*
> *the maker of heaven and earth. . . . The LORD*
> *guards you as you come and go, now and forever.*
> *Psalm 121:1–2, 8*

Your Perfect Help

"My help comes from the LORD, the maker of heaven and earth." Did you catch that? The Father God, the Alpha and Omega, the Great I AM is the source of your help. No better source of help exists anywhere.

Think of times in your life when there was no help anywhere you turned. Remember the times when you sought help from sources that just didn't provide any help at all. People disappointed you. The solutions you tried came up empty. You felt alone. At times it seemed even that God had retreated from you.

The psalmist says to fix your gaze on the majestic horizon. What you've been aching for all along lies there. Matthew 6:33 issues the perfect reminder: "First, be concerned about his kingdom and what has his approval." With your focus and trust directed heavenward, everything—yes, every single thing—will fall into place.

Do you need help with a wayward child or spouse? The Creator has a plan. Do you feel powerless in a situation at work or in the community? Your Abba Father knows it and He's got your back. Financial issues? God promises to meet your needs. As today's verse indicates, He will watch over your comings and goings and will be there to protect you. Lift your eyes to the high places today; your help is now cresting the summit.

Holy God,

it is almost hard for me to believe that the power You used to create the world is the same power that helps me find my way in it. Hallelujah! Take my face in Your holy hands and lift my eyes this very day to seek You as my perfect source of help.

Loving God,

Thank You for the gift of Your Word. Help me memorize and store it in my heart. Let it change me by shaping the way I think and act. I want to treasure You today.

I wholeheartedly searched for you. Do not let
me wander away from your commandments.
I have treasured your promise in my heart so
that I may not sin against you.
Psalm 119:10–11

Treasure God's Word

What do you treasure most? Is it a special piece of jewelry? A photograph album? A chest filled with mementos of days gone by?

Jesus spoke of treasures once when He said, "Store up treasures for yourselves in heaven, where moths and rust don't destroy and thieves don't break in and steal. Your heart will be where your treasure is" (Matthew 6:20–21). The psalmist said that he had treasured God's promise in his heart so that he would not sin.

The best way to treasure God's Word in your heart is to learn it and memorize it so that it's ready at hand when you need it. By taking a verse or two and patiently working it into your mind and heart, your responses and attitudes begin to change. They will line up with God's way of doing things.

Take an index card and write down a verse that is relevant to your life today. Put the card in your purse and carry it with you this week as you work to memorize the verse. After a short time, you'll find that God's Word will begin to saturate your mind and influence your behavior.

When you take the time and effort to memorize the Bible, it means that you treasure God's Word. And that treasure is for keeps.

*I cry out to you for help, O Lord, and in the
morning my prayer will come into your presence.*
Psalm 88:13

Morning Surrender

The freshness of a brand new morning is the perfect time to
communicate with God. C. S. Lewis wrote about the importance of prayer and surrender at the beginning of each day before
your wishes and desires rush in and take over. Lewis compared our
voices to wild animals and described the process as pushing your
voice back so to be able to hear God's other, quieter voice.

Prayer and listening take effort and intention. You learn to do
them, however, only by practicing. So this morning, as you begin
your day, talk to God. With the psalmist, let your prayer come into His
presence this morning.

Get a fresh piece of paper or a new notebook and write to God.
Thank Him for the gift of a new day and intentionally surrender it
back to His care. Make a list of the things you need or want to get
done. Then offer your list to God. Ask Him to guide your steps today
and to show you when to allow "divine appointments" to interrupt
your schedule. Allow God to design your day, and then receive His
plans gladly. Try to make this part of your morning routine.

As you leave all the day's plans to God, your perspective changes.
Stress melts away because you no longer need to control or manipulate what happens. Instead, you step into the day knowing that you
and God are on the same page, and you're walking in His will.

Heavenly Father,

help me learn to push aside my desires first thing this morning. I want to hear Your voice instead. Show me how to quiet my mind, and trust that You will create this day for me.

Lord,

I give You control of my life, my hopes and dreams and even my troubles. I ask You to be with me today. Help me to get through this storm I am facing, and lead me to the peaceful waters of the shore of your love. Bring a joyful sunset to the trouble of my day, and guide me through today's interactions with others.

If I climb upward on the rays of the morning sun
or land on the most distant shore of the sea where
the sun sets, even there your hand would guide me
and your right hand would hold on to me.
Psalm 139:9–10

The Distant Shore

What problems are you facing today? As you sip your cup of morning coffee and reflect on the tough issues you face, don't forget that the Lord's presence is inescapable; all of creation bears witness to His handiwork. God will help you navigate across the sea of your life and He'll never be too far away to rescue you from danger.

Are you stuck in the middle of what feels like a never-ending storm of strife and trouble? Heartache and pain? Illness or crisis? Do you feel like reaching out for a hand to hold, like your boat is about to tip over due to the raging waves of chaos? This verse reveals to us that the Lord is holding out His hand. The Lord is waiting for you to grab on to His strong grip and allow Him to guide you to the shore.

Psalm 139 is packed full of assurance that the Lord is present and active, no matter how wild your moments of life may seem. There's no escaping the all-powerful love of God. He's crazy about you! In your troubles, God promises to be your support, guiding you and holding you tight through life's toughest storms.

Your merciful Lord and Savior will be faithful to carry you safely to the shore, just in time to enjoy a beautiful sunset this evening. As you begin your day, have confidence in knowing that God is not only on your side but that He is guiding you and holding you tight.

> *The eternal God, the LORD, the Creator of the ends of the
> earth, doesn't grow tired or become weary. His understanding
> is beyond reach. He gives strength to those who grow tired and
> increases the strength of those who are weak. . . . The strength
> of those who wait with hope in the LORD will be renewed. They
> will soar on wings like eagles. They will run and won't become
> weary. They will walk and won't grow tired.*
> Isaiah 40:28–31

In the Starting Blocks

At a track meet, even the spectators in the stands can sense the tension the runners experience in the moments before the starter's pistol is fired. As each racer plants her feet in the starting blocks, her physical posture of readiness is the fastest, most effective way to launch into her run. Those still, expectant seconds in the blocks give the runner an opportunity to intensely focus on the course before her, until . . .

Bang! The pistol is fired and she explodes into the race.

Though a racer's job is all about motion, those moments paused and waiting in the starting blocks are essential to running her race well. Your own busy agenda holds the temptation to simply rush into your day. These moments of prayer in your morning are your opportunity to plant your feet in the starting blocks and seek God's supernatural strength and understanding for the race of your everyday life.

Offer yourself to God today, laying all of your needs, concerns and hopes at His feet, then take a few moments to simply wait on Him in silence. By first placing yourself in a posture of waiting readiness with Him, you'll be prepared to run today's race well.

Heavenly Father,

I am waiting here in the starting blocks. I am laying the weight of all my concerns for the day before You. I need Your strength to run today's race well. Give me the strength and sustenance I need.

Jesus,

without You, I am as powerless as a light bulb sitting in a package on a store shelf. I come to You this morning and acknowledge that You alone are my source. Help me to stay connected to You everywhere I go and in everything I do.

You are light for the world. . . . Let your light shine
in front of people. Then they will see the good that you
do and praise your Father in heaven.
Matthew 5:14–16

Shine On!

If you're an early riser, you probably flipped on a light in your bathroom or kitchen without thinking much about it. We are able to bring light into the darkness with such ease, aren't we?

Jesus shared the words above with an audience used to working very, very hard to generate a different kind of light in their lives. Many of His hearers longed to reflect God's goodness and purity. The only way they could dream of creating a light filled life with God was by following long lists of do's and don'ts. It was almost as if they were light bulbs trying to glow while being completely disconnected from their source of power.

Jesus turned those futile efforts upside down with His words, "You are light for the world." He wanted His hearers to know that doing good always flows out of a connection to Him, rather than trying to create a connection by performing lists of righteous acts.

You don't need to try to generate your own current. He is your power source. As you are connected to Him, you can't do anything except shine. His life automatically flows through you like electricity flows through a light bulb.

Is there a lamp or fixture near you this morning? Turn the light on for a moment and enjoy the simplicity of the bulb's glow. Connected to its power source, it shines. And today, so can you!

*Everything you say or do should be done in
the name of the Lord Jesus, giving thanks to
God the Father through him.*
Colossians 3:17

Your To-Do List

What does your "to-do" list look like for today? Are you already stressing about the time it will take you to get everything done? How are you going to do these mundane tasks "in the name of the Lord Jesus, giving thanks to God the Father"? After all, it's just a to-do list—groceries, dry cleaning, work tasks, errands. How can these possibly make a difference to Jesus?

Anything that concerns you concerns Jesus. Anything on your list today is important to Him. Yes, it may seem mundane, but if you remember who you are and why you're still walking on the planet, you'll remember that every day is a divine appointment, every task is a divine opportunity to do it in the name of Jesus.

Go to the grocery store? Maybe you'll unexpectedly meet a friend in the cereal aisle and can follow up on a prayer request from a few weeks back. Pick up dry cleaning? An opportunity to smile and thank the harried woman behind the counter. Work tasks? A chance to do your job well, help your co-workers, serve a client, meet a need. Errands? You never know what might await around the corner—even if it's an opportunity to learn patience in line at the post office!

Every step of your day can be done " in the name of the Lord Jesus." He desires that you glorify Him with every moment of your day. With Jesus, the opportunities will arise without any trouble at all.

Lord,

I commit this day to you. Please guide me through all my errands, activities, thoughts, and interactions. May You be glorified in my conversations and actions. Help me be alert for opportunities to glorify You in all I say and do.

Precious Lord,

You amaze me every single day. How like You to strengthen me with the joy I find in You. Help me to flex my joy muscle more and more, starting today, so that it becomes second nature for me to choose joy in all circumstances. There I will find Your awesome strength.

*Today is a holy day for the Lord. Don't be sad because
the joy you have in the LORD is your strength.*
Nehemiah 8:10

Flexing Your Joy Muscle

When you stretch and strain your muscles, working them
to the point of exhaustion, you can feel a "burn"—a painful
but satisfying sensation guaranteeing that when the strained muscles
heal, they will be bigger and stronger.

Just as temporary stress and strain ultimately produce strength
in muscles, life's stresses and strains can ultimately result in spiritual
strength. Even though it seems the weight of the world is almost
unbearable, a heavenly hand wants to cup your elbow and help you
lift the heavy burden. That's the joy of the Lord—a power source that
is always available to give you the strength that you need.

Claim today as holy for the Lord, just as Nehemiah told the
Israelites. The people had just heard the Word of the Lord read aloud
and they were weeping as they realized how far they had strayed
from God. That was a good thing, but Nehemiah didn't want them to
weep, to feel guilty, to give up in depression. He challenged them to
find joy in the God who still loved them and was drawing them back
to Himself. He challenged them to let that joy give them strength to
move forward, living as God wanted them to live.

God's joy will give you strength as well. Let the joy of the Lord flow
through every part of you today as you and He carry your burdens
together.

Almighty LORD, you made heaven and earth
by your great strength and powerful arm.
Nothing is too hard for you.
Jeremiah 32:17

Tying Together

It's too hard! There's no way I can do this! Do those thoughts ever reverberate through your mind?

Think back to when you were learning to tie your shoes. Your sweet chubby child's fingers were awkward as they tried to create that impossible bow. Time and time again you tried to imitate the adult who effortlessly, almost magically, created perfectly symmetrical bunny ears and ends of the right length out of nothing more than dangly strings.

Maybe you mastered "criss-cross applesauce" right away, but once past the bunny ears, everything seemed to fall apart. Frustration churned as you saw the result of your clumsy attempts. Perhaps you even declared defeat, vowing you'd wear Velcro shoes forever!

And yet, sweet friend, here you are today—able to tie your shoes! Continued practice coupled with a humble willingness to follow someone else's lead—someone who'd mastered the task—finally allowed you to reach your goal.

Now you have new goals. Are you caring for an aging parent? Is your chosen profession on hold? Is your marriage a daily struggle? Keep plugging away and follow the lead of the Master. Nothing is too hard for Him. Not one thing. Allow Him to work His mighty strength and power through precious, chosen you. Feel His agile hands guide your uneasy fingers as He helps you tie up your loose ends today.

Father,

nothing is too hard for You! I invite You into every situation in my life in which I feel powerless and defeated. Guide my actions as I surrender to You in complete faith that You'll tie everything up according to Your master plan.

A Heavenly Father

I love You. I am Your child. Thank You for wrapping your arms around me this morning as I prepare for the day ahead. Walk with me, talk with me, guide me. May I never lose the childlike sense of wonder at Your constant care for me.

*Consider this: The Father has given us his love.
He loves us so much that we are actually called
God's dear children. And that's what we are.*
1 John 3:1

God's Daughter

Remember when life seemed uncomplicated? If you think back, you'll realize that a time once existed when a pretty red dress that billowed when you danced could make you the happiest little girl alive.

Where did those times go?

As much as those carefree days would be a welcome respite from the ups and downs of life today, it's also true that walking with God through the mountains and valleys of life has drawn you closer to Him. How much more do you know about Him because of where you've been together? How much more do you love Him because you've seen over and over how much He loves you?

This morning you continue your journey with your loving heavenly Father. You are a woman of God, but you are still His child—wide-eyed with wonder at His awesome presence and filled with joy at the truth of His promises. No matter what hurts or heartaches have come your way, your heavenly Father gathers you in His arms to comfort and strengthen you for the day ahead.

Yes, life is complex and complicated, but one simple truth cuts through all the static: You are a precious daughter of God.

Put on something red and rejoice in the love of your Father in heaven.

Take to heart these words that I give you today. Repeat them to your children. Talk about them when you're at home or away, when you lie down or get up.

Deuteronomy 6:6–7

Important Talk

Ever heard the comment that women talk more than men? It's not politically correct these days to say it, but studies reveal that women consistently use more words in a day than men do.

Accept the way God designed you and enjoy the fact that talking to family and friends generally comes easy. However, it would be wise to distinguish between "just talking" and "important talk." In other words, those many words you use in a day should be more than just chatter. In fact, the command of Deuteronomy 6 is that some of those daily words should be from God's Word—His commands and promises repeated to those around us, at home or away, when lying down or getting up.

The verses specifically mention children, and if you're a mom, you know the importance of sharing God's Word with your kids. More than that, however, God gives you various places, people, and opportunities to share His words throughout your day, either as instruction or encouragement to others. As a friend, you may be the only one who encourages another woman today with the Word of God. "Like golden apples in silver settings, so is a word spoken at the right time" (Proverbs 25:11).

How will your words help your children today? Your husband? Your friends? Your co-workers? Ask that God take charge of the many words you will use today.

All-wise Father

I'm grateful to be Your
child. Thank You for the
comfort of Your words.
Remind me throughout
this day to not only take
to heart Your words, but
to share them with my
children and friends.

✦Thank You,

my faithful Lord, for going
with me whatever I face.
Sometimes life's trials
and struggles make me
afraid. They look so large.
And I know that problems
look large when I take
my eyes off the Problem
Solver. Today, give me the
strength and courage to
keep my focus on You.

Be strong and courageous. Don't tremble! Don't be afraid
of them! The LORD your God is the one who is going with
you. He won't abandon you or leave you.
Deuteronomy 31:6

Never Alone

One of the largest but irrational fears of early childhood is abandonment. Little children don't realize they carry this fear, but it's behind some of their behavior and is especially evident when they go through separation anxiety.

Some adults still carry that fear. Perhaps as children, they were left behind in a school field trip, felt neglected by an emotionally absent parent, were ostracized by their peers, or were literally abandoned by those who should have cared for them. Those hard events make permanent impressions on the wet cement of the soul.

The good news is that God will never leave or forsake you. Nothing can separate you from His love. Did you awake this morning already burdened with a heavy load? Are you facing problems that you just don't know how to handle? Whatever you're facing, God knows. He surrounds you—His precious possession. He stands ready and able to provide love, assurance, wisdom, and help. You are not alone. You've never been alone.

This bright, new morning, revel in the fact that God is your all-knowing teacher, faithful friend, and loving parent. His enormous affection for you means He will never abandon or leave you. Today, believe in His protection and provision. Be strong and courageous. Step into your day knowing that "God is the one who is going with you."

Let my teachings come down like raindrops. Let my
words drip like dew, like gentle rain on grass, like
showers on green plants.
Deuteronomy 32:2

Soul Refreshment

How refreshing is the Word of the Lord! The Father wants His
Word to be soothing and nourishing. He wants His teachings to "come down like raindrops"—refreshing, cleansing, satisfying,
just like your morning shower.

But sometimes it doesn't seem that way. You may at times feel that
your devotions seem stale, your prayer time feels perfunctory, you're
not feeling refreshed by God's Word at all. What can you do to enliven
this time with God so that you come away feeling freshly showered?
Perhaps it's a question of immersion. You don't get fully clean by
sticking just your toe in the shower. You won't get the full effect of
God's Word until you're immersed in it, until the teachings come
down like raindrops around you.

God's Word is often compared to water, that most valuable and
wholesome resource. Remember the blessed man that the psalmist
praises in Psalm 1. The study of God's law, the Word of the Lord,
makes this man "like a tree planted beside streams—a tree that
produces fruit in season and whose leaves do not wither" (Psalm 1:3).
The psalmist knows that a diligent study of the Word of God helps
him produce fruit and keeps him from withering.

Remember that the Father wants His teachings to refresh you. Let
today be one of the days when His Word is as soothing as "showers
on green plants."

Father,

let Your teaching be as refreshing as soft rain showers. Thank You for blessing me with Your Word, which will continue to strengthen me through both good days and bad.

God of the sunrise,

You are so faithful to me
and so remarkable in the
ways You reveal Yourself
to me. Today let me shine
for You like the rising
sun, signaling to others
Your presence. Help me
illuminate the world with
Your glory.

> *May those who love the LORD be like the sun*
> *when it rises in all its brightness.*
> *Judges 5:31*

Shine Brightly

Watching the sun rise is a beautiful moment of the day. You feel privileged to see the sun emerge from behind the horizon, changing the landscape with its presence. Some sunrises are breathtaking. Vibrant colors spread across the sky, filling the morning with joy. Other sunrises are simple, without the explosions of color, but peaceful and calm. Both are beautiful in their own unique ways, for they usher in the promise of a new day. A sunrise reminds us of many of God's characteristics: His love for beauty, faithfulness which knows no end, and His grace that allows us to begin anew each day. The light of the sunrise points to our powerful, amazing God.

As the sun "rises in all its brightness," it shines on a waking world. Whether you can see the sunrise through your window or not, the image is beautiful. But even more important than the image is the spirit with which the author of this verse writes. The author is blessing you with these words, praying that you can be as remarkable and faithful as the sunrise.

As someone who cherishes the Lord, you can be like the rising sun, which inspires hope for the new day. You can be like the sunrise that points to God's beauty, faithfulness, and grace. And, like the sunrise, you can communicate God's warm love to the people in your world today.

God arms me with strength His perfect way sets me free. He makes my feet like those of a deer and gives me sure footing on high places.
2 Samuel 22:33–34

Firm Footing

Mountain goats are astonishing creatures. They prance around mountain ledges upon which any human would be frozen in terror. They scamper on cliffs high on a mountain side and seem to be perfectly comfortable in situations that, to us, appear dreadfully dangerous. God created mountain goats with feet that put our best climbing innovations to shame. Cloven in two and spread wide to increase balance, their hooves are also roughly padded, allowing their feet to maintain a grip on treacherous terrain.

Perhaps you are no stranger to a treacherous environment, a dangerous situation, a high place where you are very unsure of your footing. Perhaps that's the path that is set before you today. Even in this terrain, however, you can rejoice in the Lord: His promises are true. He is a shield that protects you. He is your rock, your strength, and your freedom.

As you walk your path today, remember that God promises the sure footing of the mountain goat so that you can balance on the high, dangerous places without a turned ankle, a stumble, or a slip. You can walk without fear of falling. Although you may look over the precipice and be filled with apprehension, turn your eyes back to the One who promises to never let you stumble or fall.

God,

I pray that today You will arm me with Your strength. May Your perfect way set my spirit free to do Your will. I hold fast to the promise that You direct my steps and keep me from falling, slipping, or failing. Just as You have in the past, show me how Your promises for my life are true.

❧ *Lord,*

sometimes it is really difficult for me to wait. I know that I am impatient. I know that my heart is restless. Thank You for reminding me that I need to wait for You and that in my waiting You will meet me, You will teach me, and You will grow me into someone more like You. Help me to be patient enough to wait for You.

Make your ways known to me, O LORD, and teach me
your paths. Lead me in your truth and teach me because
you are God, my savior. I wait all day long for you.
Psalm 25:4–5

Waiting to Fly

When asking for directions, do you leave before you're given all the turns and signposts you need to watch for? When setting up new electronic equipment, do you read halfway through the instructions and then "wing it"—just hoping that you don't fry something when you turn it on? Of course not. Yet how often we lose patience when it comes to waiting for answers to prayer, how often we decide we're just going to wing it and hope for the best.

Answers to prayer do not often come immediately. Like the caterpillar in the chrysalis, waiting can be a long process. And yet, in your waiting, God will work in your heart in hidden ways. The beauty of the monarch's wings can only emerge after waiting for the right time. If the monarch emerges too soon, the wings will be spoiled and the butterfly will never fly.

Are you willing to believe that what God wants for you is far superior to anything that you could want for yourself? Are you willing to wait? While you wait God will grow you. While you wait He will meet you. While you wait you learn about sacrifice.

And how long must you wait? Does it really matter? God loves you. It is in this time of waiting that He will make His ways known to you, He will lead you in His truth, He will teach you.

That makes the waiting worthwhile.

Entrust your ways to the LORD. Trust him,
and he will act on your behalf.
He will make your righteousness shine like a light,
your just cause like the noonday sun.
Psalm 37:5–6

Commanding Voices

Sometimes you may get the feeling that everyone has ideas for your life: do this activity, try that product, become this kind of a woman. These suggestions bombard you from all sides. Try as hard as you may, you can never follow all of these commands. What's more, you will never be happy listening to all of these voices that tell you conflicting things to do.

At your first reading of these verses, you might think the author is just as bossy as the people of this world. After all, the author commands you to do many things, all listed in a very short space! You are told to trust the Lord, do good things, live in the land, practice being faithful, be happy with the Lord, and entrust your ways to Him. It's almost as overwhelming as flipping through a magazine, looking only at the advertisements and self-help articles. But when you look at the passage again, the commands the author exhorts you to obey are encouraging and affirming. Why? Because when you trust in Him, He "will give you the desires of your heart," "will act on your behalf," and "will make your righteousness shine like a light, your just cause like the noonday sun."

When you trust the Lord and do good, you become a bright light in a dark world.

Father God,

I ask that these words from Psalm 37 will echo in my head. Help me to follow these suggestions for my life. I know that my trust in You and the living out of my faith will completely change me. Thank You for knowing my heart and for promising to fulfill it completely. Let me shine for You today.

Dearest Lord, thank You so much for this new day. Thank You for caring about me individually. Help me to never take You for granted but to always be awed by Your creation and Your work in me. I will live this and every day for You.

Those who live at the ends of the earth are in awe of your miraculous signs. The lands of the morning sunrise and evening sunset sing joyfully.

Psalm 65:8

Sunrise, Sunset

An elderly man once remarked that when he woke each morning, he checked to see which side of the sod he was on and found it miraculous that he was still on the top.

How do you respond to the arrival of each new morning? Are you amazed by each new day you've been granted or do you roll over, hit the snooze button, and growl at anyone or anything that disturbs you?

Wherever you are, you are living in a miracle. Think about it: When the sun is rising for you, it is setting for those on the opposite side of the globe. The wondrous sunrise you experience is a sunset for someone else, thousands of miles away. How many people are, all at once, gazing in awe at the miracle of one day, both beginning and ending?

And, in the midst of the millions who praise Him, God cares for you. He knows your name and hears your prayers!

Puts things into perspective, doesn't it? Rather than just checking the sod, make a point of praising God for something new each day. Look out your window and allow yourself to be awed by His creation. Don't just hit the snooze button! Find joy in this morning's sunrise, and be thankful for the gift of another day to live for Him.

*Do not be afraid, because I have reclaimed you. I have
called you by name; you are mine. When you go through
the sea, I am with you. When you go through rivers, they
will not sweep you away.*
Isaiah 43:1–2

Calling Your Name

This morning, the Lord reminds you: "I have called you by
name; you are mine." Let your unsettled heart be calmed, let
your fears and loneliness cease. He whispers to you, His daughter, "Do
not be afraid, because I have reclaimed you." You were His once, but
you were torn apart in sin from Him. But He has brought you back to
Himself because of His great love—"I have reclaimed you," He says,
"you are mine."

What precious promises—that the God of the universe would
reach down to touch your soul this morning with His reminder of
how much you mean to Him. And beyond that, He promises never
to leave you, never to let you face difficulty alone. The trials of life will
come, but He will be with you. When you go through the storms on
the sea, battered by circumstances and worry, He is with you, protecting you, holding you above the threatening waves to keep you from
going under. When the river's current makes you afraid that you'll
never be able to stand without being knocked over, He will hold you
close and keep you from being swept away. When you must walk
through the scathing fire of criticism, anger, or pain, you will emerge
without burns, without harm.

Whether you're facing a raging sea, a swift-flowing river, or a
scorching fire, God places your hand in His and says, "I am with you.
We can walk through this together."

Dearest Lord,

Your faithfulness toward me is awesome. You have reclaimed me; I am Yours! You will never forsake me, not in the sea, not in the river's swift current, not in the midst of the fire. I am Yours because of Your kindness toward me. Hold my hand tightly as we walk together today.

Lord,

You are the master of the sun and of the moon, but the day is coming when You will be the only source of light. I ask that You illuminate my life today, giving me wisdom to deal with the things You show me. Nourish my soul, warm my heart, guide my steps by Your light today.

The sun will no longer be your light during the day, nor will the brightness of the moon give you light, but the LORD will be your everlasting light. Your God will be your glory.

Isaiah 60:19

A Light to Live By

Sundials are both beautiful and fascinating. They appear almost like works of art—designed with precision and strategically placed in lush surroundings such as a garden full of sunlight. You probably have never needed to master the art of telling time on a sundial, but you know the basics: The sun casts a shadow from the centerpiece onto the dial where someone skilled could discern a general time of the day. As the earth turned and the sun swept across the sky, the shadow moved around the dial.

Most sundials today are simply placed for looks since most people use more modern methods of time-telling. However, the world still depends on the regularity of the sun to order its days. Plant life, animal life, people, and all of nature count on the movements of the sun and the moon to regulate our time, to move the tides, to change the seasons.

There will be a time, though, when the sun and the moon will no longer shine. No longer will they dictate when you rise and when you sleep. At one point in the future, the Lord will literally become your "everlasting light."

As the sun rises this morning, thank the Lord that He promises to be the source of everlasting light through all eternity. Thank Him that today He is your spiritual light—nourishing you, warming you, guiding you.

I know the plans that I have for you, declares the LORD. They are plans for peace and not disaster, plans to give you a future filled with hope. Then you will call to me. You will come and pray to me, and I will hear you.
Jeremiah 29:11–12

Stormy Weather

Open your calendar or your pocket planner and take a look at today's schedule. What activities crowd your day? Scan the next few weeks or months. Chances are you have plans jotted in—an appointment here, a meeting there, a vacation week penciled in over here. Your life is neatly planned out and you pretty much know what to expect out of today and the coming days.

But what do you do when your neatly-planned schedule gets blown off course? The unexpected stormy wind whips through your planned-out sunny day. You catch a bad sickness and end up in bed for a few days; a family member needs your help; a sudden turn of events takes your life and turns it upside down.

Even though you might enjoy a change from your routine once in a while, you probably don't relish sudden, unexpected, life-altering events. But, as you can probably already attest, these things happen. When faced with these unexpected storms, you can be assured that God already has the way planned for you. He knows what today will bring, whether that particular event is on your schedule or not.

God's plans for you are the best. As He told Jeremiah, His plans are for peace, not disaster. His plans are to give you a future filled with hope. So when your days are sunny, cloudless, and go exactly as planned, give thanks. And when the unexpected storm arrives, handle it gracefully, and thank God that He is in control.

Dearest Lord,

thank You for being in
control. Help me never
forget that You know
what will happen in my
life every day, and that
Your plans for me are
good. You are my future
and hope.

Lord Jesus,

I invite You to live in me today and every day. I desire that marvelous co-mingling of our spirits, so that all I do bears fruit for You and Your Kingdom. Come, let's dwell together, my precious Savior, all the days of my life.

Live in me, and I will live in you.
A branch cannot produce any fruit by itself.
It has to stay attached to the vine. In the same way,
you cannot produce fruit unless you live in me.
John 15:4

Fruit of the Vine

You're ambling along a vineyard, swinging a basket and peering among the branches for the ripest, plumpest fruit. Many grapes are still greenish so you leave them to mature. But then you spy a particularly bountiful area and move in, anticipating the delightful thump of each cluster as it lands in your basket. You can't help but sample one savory specimen and as the juice bursts onto your tongue, you appreciate the gift of fruit ripened to perfection in its due season.

Squatting to reach a low cluster, however, you notice a branch that has snapped, perhaps by a violent wind. What a shame, you think, noticing that what once held so much potential now yields only dead fruit, brown and shriveled, that will benefit no one. Being cut off from its supply of life-giving sustenance, the branch has withered and died, no longer able to do what it was created to do.

Do you ever feel like that dried up branch? Jesus clearly teaches that apart from Him all labor is in vain. If you want a life that bears lasting fruit, you must stay connected to Him, your life source.

At the joint where branch meets vine, there's a lovely co-mingling of your humanity and His supernatural divinity; they coalesce to give birth to beautiful fruit just dripping with His sweet goodness—today and every day for the rest of your life.

Don't you know that you are God's temple
and that God's Spirit lives in you?
1 Corinthians 3:16

God's Temple

Solomon built one. Zerubbabel built one. You are one—
a living temple fashioned and crafted by God Himself.
Ancient temples used gold, silver, and precious metals as symbols
of purity and holiness; they were places people believed their gods
lived. Solomon's magnificent temple (read about it in 1 Kings 6) and
Zerubbabel's temple (a rebuilding of Solomon's temple after its destruction by the Babylonians—see 2 Kings 25 and Ezra 3) were places
for God's presence among His people. However, with Christ came a
new living temple made of people who believe in Him and who are
made beautiful by the presence of the Holy Spirit within each one.

Maybe this morning you don't feel like a beautiful temple of God.
The past casts shadows around every nook and cranny—whether
from bad choices, poor decisions, or costly mistakes. Seasons of neglect or strife have caused crumbling walls or a cracking foundation.

No matter what you have built in your life before, today is a new
day! A day to be renewed and encouraged, knowing that the Holy
Spirit is there with you, beside you, in you. He is ready and waiting to
be your source of strength and hope this day, especially in the middle
of your challenges. Choose today to be a living temple founded
on Christ and transformed by the Holy Spirit—a place of character
where God resides, a place of beauty where God is reflected, a place
of sanctuary where God is welcomed.

Thank You,

God, for the gift of Your Son and the Holy Spirit. Help me to remember that I am part of something bigger than myself   Your holy, living temple. Give me wisdom and strength today to build up Your temple, remembering that I am beautiful and precious in Your sight.

Dear Lord,

come with me as I tackle my to-do list today. Help me to see each task –even eating and drinking—as an opportunity to glorify You by being content and self-controlled. How I want to feel Your pleasure as I submit all I do to Your glory.

*So, whether you eat or drink, or whatever you do,
do everything to the glory of God.*
1 Corinthians 10:31

Bask in the Task

Rolling out of bed this morning, did your task list infiltrate your thoughts? Did it cross your mind what a drag it can be just keeping up with the daily grind? It's so easy to feel caught in a rut since the details of life can seem menial and sometimes meaningless.

But God desires joy for you amidst those ruts. In fact, you can bring Him glory there. As today's verse indicates, what you do sometimes matters much less to God than how you do it.

Anyone can wipe down the kitchen for the third time in one day, but not everyone can do it while rockin' a praise song.

Anyone can re-do a project at work because the boss gave the wrong instructions the first time, but not everyone can do it without grumbling.

Anyone can go elbow deep in the toilet to work on a rust stain, but many aren't willing to do it at all, much less happily.

As undignified or "un-fun" as some tasks seem, they can bring glory to God if you approach them with a servant's heart. Remember Jesus illustrating this to the disciples by washing their filthy feet? And yet He was happy to do it.

Now you—purposefully chosen you—are being used to bless others who might not even show appreciation. But dear one, rest assured: There's One beaming down at you, pleased at your willingness to do all things for His glory. Can you feel His pleasure?

I also pray that love may be the ground into which you sink your roots and on which you have your foundation. This way, with all of God's people you will be able to understand how wide, long, high, and deep his love is.

Ephesians 3:17–18

Rooted in Love

When the apostle Paul wanted to describe believers' relationship with God, he drew upon the powerful image of roots sunk deep into the ground. A magnificent tree stands tall only because of a deep and wide root system that provides a strong solid foundation against the storms as well as nourishment from deep in the soil.

The metaphor of the roots beautifully portrays the relationship you should have with the love of Christ: Christ's love holds you fast in the midst of storms and nourishes you constantly. Like a tree, you can choose to be constantly sinking the roots of your life into Christ's foundational love. The deeper you root yourself in Him, the less likely you will be upturned by life's storms. By being rooted in Christ's love, you will find yourself filled with God. You will begin to understand "how wide, long, high, and deep his love is." You find that it surrounds you—you can't get over it, around it, under it, or through it. His love is a hedge around you in ways that go beyond your ability to understand. And the more you learn about Christ's love, the more you become filled up with Him.

Like a tree standing tall in the forest, send your roots deep into Christ's love. Ask Him to fill you up today with His amazing love.

Our Loving God

I praise You for providing this love as my foundation. This is a love I can grow into and sink into, a love that will forever change me. Fill me with Yourself as Your love nourishes my soul.

Dear Jesus,

You know that sometimes my heart doesn't sing to You. Sometimes my heart grumbles and complains. But Jesus, I trust that You will put a song in my head and in my heart today. Let it stick in my thoughts and remind me of Your presence in my life.

*Let Christ's word with all its wisdom and richness live in you.
Use psalms, hymns, and spiritual songs to teach and instruct
yourselves about God's kindness. Sing to God in your hearts.*
Colossians 3:16

Songs in the Heart

Songs have a remarkable way of filling our minds. Melodies
meander around the edge of your subconscious while you
go about your day. They repeat endlessly, permeating your thoughts
with catchy choruses, clever snippets, and melodic tunes. You can
be concentrating on other things when suddenly a line comes out
of your mouth. This is potentially embarrassing (especially around
strangers), but the embarrassment doesn't stop the song reverberat-
ing through your head.

It's no wonder, then, that you are encouraged to let Christ's word
live in you through songs. And better to sing a song endlessly than to
let your heart grow downtrodden. Worshiping through song can be a
powerful connection with God. The apostle Paul encouraged the Co-
lossian believers to have "psalms, hymns, and spiritual songs" ringing
through their heads, sticking in their minds with tenacity, for along
with those melodies would come Christ's word in all its wisdom and
richness. Singing to God in your head will certainly carry over to your
heart, allowing God to have an active presence in your life. As you
sing the songs in your heart throughout the day, you will have God's
kindness and wisdom dwelling in you.

So don't be afraid to sing! Your best audience is God, and He loves
to hear you!

Every good present and every perfect gift comes from above, from the Father who made the sun, moon, and stars. The Father doesn't change like the shifting shadows produced by the sun and the moon.

James 1:17

His Presence in Presents

Think back to your birthdays when you were a little girl. Can you remember trying to harness your anticipation until you thought you were going to burst? You knew that those beautifully-wrapped presents had been chosen carefully just for you and when you were finally allowed to tear into the wrapping paper, you were overjoyed at what was inside! There were some items from your list as well as some better-than-imagined surprises. Your parents knew how to delight their precious daughter.

And so does Someone else. Just think how even more perfect the gifts are that God showers on you. Matthew 7:11 says, "Even though you're evil, you know how to give good gifts to your children. So how much more will your Father in heaven give good things to those who ask him?" He provides every good and perfect gift and His desire to do so never changes.

What presents has God already given you? Imagine Him happily planning the details of surprising you with them, smiling at your reaction. And He's not finished yet! Begin to look forward to—just as you did during those childhood birthdays—what He has in store for you, His precious daughter. As you spend today with your heavenly Father, allow yourself to get lost in the giddiness of anticipating what perfect gift He's wrapping up just for you.

Lord,

thank You for devoting the same power that created the heavenly bodies into marvelous gifts You've crafted specifically for me. They are good even beyond my understanding. Thank You for Your steadfast faithfulness and perfection in showing me Your love.

Dear Lord,

make me an example of
Your love today to every-
one I encounter. I rejoice
that You have allowed
more time for those
who are seeking You to
find You. Thank You for
another day.

Dear friends, don't ignore this fact: One day with the Lord is like
a thousand years, and a thousand years are like one day.
2 Peter 3:8

Tick Tock

Hollywood does a good job of making time travel seem extraordinarily commonplace. Whether riding in a DeLorean or a stepping through a wardrobe, people have been able to travel in time—for better or for worse.

In these verses, Peter is not spilling the cosmic secret to altering the space-time continuum. Rather, he's giving a glimpse of the infinite and eternal God. Because He has always existed and always will exist, time itself means very little to Him. Because you are on this earth for only a limited amount of time, however, every minute counts. You live your life by the clock—there is a time when you arise in the morning, times when you eat, work, play, exercise, do your devotions, go to church, go to bed . . .

So you might wonder, what is it all for, anyway, this daily routine which recycles every 24 hours? Why can't Jesus return as He promised and take you to be with Him in heaven, ending this boring, merry-go-round existence?

The answer is in verse 9: He is being patient, allowing others the opportunity to repent and come to know Him, just as you know Him.

So when you wake up and the cycle begins again, rejoice. Pray for those whom you might influence today for Christ. Think of those who will come to salvation this very day. After all, that is the only reason the cycle continues.

God is faithful and reliable. If we confess our sins, he forgives them and cleanses us from everything we've done wrong.
1 John 1:9

Cleansing Confession

Confessing your sins is probably not the first thing that springs to mind as you roll out of bed in the morning. You may automatically turn on the coffeepot, or maybe throw on clothes to exercise. But confessing your sins? That may seem like more of an end-of-the-day ritual, something to do after you've snapped at a family member, complained about a co-worker, or yearned after someone else's possessions.

In the morning, however, you may see more clearly some of the events of yesterday that cause you to wince into your coffee cup this morning. You may see your anxiety, your anger, or your selfishness more clearly when given the perspective of this new morning. While it's not good to dwell on the past, if you do find issues that need some cleansing—before God and perhaps before someone you may have wronged—then now is the time to do it. Ask for God's forgiveness and make a plan to ask that person's forgiveness if needed.

As you ask for forgiveness, take comfort in this promise that God is faithful and reliable to cleanse you from everything you've done wrong. Like cleansing water, He will wash away your sins, just as He has every other time. He will cleanse you from everything you've done wrong. He will give you the strength to avoid repeating that sin in this new day.

Confess and refresh. Now that's something to smile about!

Lord,

I have sinned, many times in many areas of my life. I acknowledge my sin in these areas, and I pray that You will forgive them. Make me clean in Your sight, and cleanse me from my mistakes. I praise You for Your forgiveness, Lord, which You always extend to me.

Heavenly Father,

I am here before You in a posture of humility. I am powerless to change the situation that is capturing my thoughts this morning. Simply put, I need Your help. I am depending on You and You only to come to my aid, just as Your Word promises.

There's no one like your God, Jeshurun! He rides through the heavens to help you. In majesty he rides through the clouds.
Deuteronomy 33:26

Help Is On the Way

Your phone rings. A good friend who recently moved cross-country is on the line. She is in the midst of a serious family health crisis and needs practical help: childcare, household assistance, meals. She doesn't yet know anyone in her town, and she's over-whelmed with all that must be done to keep her household running over the next several days.

More than anything, you want to be there to help, but your own family or job responsibilities keep you tethered in your current loca-tion. Though you know your friend appreciates your support and your commitment to intercede for her family, you wish you could do more.

You wish you could be there.

Moses wanted his people to know that when they needed help, they could call on God and He would come to their aid. His words portray a rescuer racing across time and space to provide the help they needed. Moses used the term "Jeshurun" here, a term of affec-tion for Israel. He wanted his beloved nation to know that God would be there. All they had to do was ask and He would ride across the heavens and through the clouds to get to them.

Our unchanging God is there for each one of us who calls Him Lord. No matter whether it is the need of your distant friend, or a need much closer to home in your own life, God's help is on the way.

*Aaron must burn sweet-smelling incense on this altar every
morning when he takes care of the lamps.*
Exodus 30:7

A Spotless Light

In the early 1900s, people used oil lamps with round glass globes to provide light for a dark room. When the glass became blackened from smoke, the globe would be carefully removed and the soot wiped off. This cleaning became almost a daily routine. Every morning they had a choice whether to clean their lamp or wait until later. If cleaning was postponed, the light would grow dim, and the lamp would be useless in the nighttime.

Notice that as the worship at the tabernacle was instituted, God told Moses that Aaron was to take care of the lamps every morning, rather than only once a week or every other week. Everything having to do with worship at the tabernacle had to be done according to God's specifics. None of the rituals could be neglected. So Aaron would have to be disciplined about maintaining the lamps.

The oil lamp can be a metaphor for life. How can you keep your lamp clean and maintain a sweet-smelling relationship with the Lord? While God will provide the cleansing, it's up to us to ask Him to reveal and wash away any sin in our lives.

Determine how you can be a spotless light for the Lord that shines brilliantly in the darkness around you. Go to God this morning and let Him wipe off any darkness that has accumulated so you can be a light before Him today.

Lord,

grant me the grace
and humility to go
to You every day—
especially when I am
in need of cleansing.
Let my life be a sweet-
smelling aroma to
You and all those
around me.

Father,

I am being prompted this morning about an area of my life characterized by inertia. I have neglected Your work and Your ways in this area. Please forgive me, and help me to move forward with You, step by step, from this moment.

> *Early in the morning Hezekiah gathered the leaders of the*
> *city and went to the LORD's temple.*
> 2 Chronicles 29:20

Life in Motion

Do you remember learning about the principle of inertia in science class? An object at rest tends to remain at rest; an object in motion tends to remain in motion. It takes an applied force greater than the object to disrupt an object's inertia. A soccer ball will sit immobile on the playing field until a well-aimed kick sets it into motion.

God's people had experienced generations of spiritual inertia when Hezekiah became king seven centuries before Christ's birth. The Bible tells us Hezekiah was a godly man: "He did what the LORD considered right, as his ancestor David had done" (2 Chronicles 29:2). Hezekiah is remembered for his willingness to interrupt generations of apathy and compromise and for returning Israel to single-minded worship of God. He focused on repairing the nation's place of worship and on encouraging his people to recommit themselves to God.

After generations of neglect, it took a surprisingly short amount of time for the people to accomplish these tasks. Hezekiah's decision halted his people's inertia. When all was in readiness, Hezekiah invited his leaders to join him in worship at the dawn of a new day. Renewal came to the nation.

Is there an area of your life that has suffered from spiritual neglect? Today you can commit to return to God in this area.

When he tests me, I'll come out as pure as gold. I have followed his footsteps closely. I have stayed on his path and did not turn from it. I have not left his commands behind. I have treasured his words in my heart.
Job 23:10–12

No Matter What

Picture this: You're running late for an appointment and can't find your glasses. You dig through your purse, the pocket of the coat you wore yesterday, and between the couch cushions. When they don't materialize, you rush through the house frantically looking everywhere for your missing specs. Fifteen frustrating minutes pass, and you reach for your cell phone to let the person you're meeting know that you're running late. And there they are . . . sitting right where you had put them so you wouldn't forget where they were.

Most of us are prone to the temptation to run here and there looking for a solution when we're in the midst of a challenging situation. Job had experienced one extremely intense test after another, and his wife and friends encouraged him to do something to put an end to the fiery trials (as if he could). Job refused, knowing that the "solutions" suggested to him by others would send him running in a dozen wrong directions. So, he would stay the course and trust God no matter what happened.

Are you going through a trial right now? Have well-meaning friends and family members suggested solutions to you that would send you running in a direction God has not called you to go? In the stillness of these moments with the Lord before you launch into your day, affirm your willingness to stay on His path, and walk according to His Word no matter what happens.

Lord,

like Job,
Your Word
tells me that trials
are designed to build
perseverance in me so
that I become mature
in my faith. Help me to
cherish Your Word and
cling to You, no mat-
ter what.

❧ *God,*

while I'm grateful that You offer Yourself as my hiding place, I don't always take You at Your word. I hide in other places. But You, O God, are my true hiding place.

Let all godly people pray to you when you may be found. Then raging
floodwater will not reach them. You are my hiding place. You protect me
from trouble. You surround me with joyous songs of salvation.
Psalm 32:6–7

Your Protector

A small child stumbles and falls down on the front porch. She picks herself up and runs to Mama weeping. Mama scoops up the youngster, examines the injury and holds her close. What a picture of comfort. You can just imagine how the child feels: safe and protected.

When difficulties arise and raging floodwaters flow around you, where do you go to find peace and comfort? David, the writer of Psalm 32, suggests a place of refuge—one that he sought many times in his life. This place of refuge is easily accessed by prayer.

When trouble comes your way, whether it is a small puddle or a monsoon of violent downpour, God can protect you. He will listen to your sorrows and hold you close in His big, strong arms. His love can give you strength to step out into the world again, braver and stronger than before. His songs will lift your soul from doubt and confusion. The Lord can even instruct you, just like a mother instructs her child. He can teach you what to do and where you should go. His eyes never lose sight of you.

So like the small child, run to your protector. Run to Jesus when you fall. He will scoop you up and hold you close.

> God is our refuge and strength, an ever-present help in
> times of trouble. . . . The LORD of Armies is with us. The
> God of Jacob is our stronghold.
> Psalm 46:1, 7

A Mighty Fortress

The newspapers and televised news stories show pictures of
war-torn areas. But sometimes a home or an office building
can be a place of war, thanks to misunderstandings and grievances.
Various types of battles await each of us daily. Interpersonal conflicts
(such as troubles with a co-worker or spouse) make everyday life a
war zone because relationships test our faith. In reality, our enemies
are not physical, but spiritual (see, for example, Ephesians 6:10–12).
The battle is for our hearts.

Fights with family members or co-workers make us want to retreat
into a safe environment. But if home itself is a war-zone, we might
try to protect ourselves from pain by erecting barriers around our
hearts. We know these to be defense mechanisms which take the
form of sarcasm, humor (laughing to ignore the pain), silence, and
other behaviors. But God's refuge is stronger than any walls we might
build up around our hearts. As the psalmist suggests, God's strength
provides a formidable barrier against the worries of this world. Only
He can provide a fortress for our hearts.

Today, you can face the battles of life knowing you are safe in
God's fortress and that you fight with His loaned strength. When
things get overwhelming this morning, close your eyes and envision
His fortress of love surrounding you. You are not fighting this battle
alone.

Lord,

thank You that I can rest
in Your protection and
find peace in Your fortress
today.

Father,
You are strong enough to carry every worry that besets me. Today I will put my trust in Your great strength. Help me to know You more every day.

*The LORD, the only true God, has spoken. He has summoned
the earth from where the sun rises to where it sets.*

Psalm 50:1

The Immensity of the Father

How magnificent is your God! This morning, dwell upon His vast power and the capability of His benevolent hands. As the psalmist proclaims, only the Lord could claim the earth as a witness of His trustworthiness to keep a covenant. If He seems too vast for comprehension, study His many names and be encouraged. He is God Almighty (Genesis 17:1), Wonderful Counselor and Prince of Peace (Isaiah 9:6), Abba (Mark 14:36), Father (Luke 11:2). The names of your Father allow you to see the facets of His character. As you study His names, watch His greatness spread out before you each day, even as you come to know Him more intimately.

The character of your heavenly Father is like that of the ocean—vast, awe-inspiring, powerful. Every day the sea is renewed before your eyes and the longer you watch, the better you come to know it. It is pearly and calm on a mild spring dawn, brilliantly blue under the summer sun, wild and foaming in a winter storm, and glowing silver beneath a rising moon. You cannot know the character of the Father at a glance, but you can know Him more each day simply by being with Him. Trust Him to reveal Himself to you.

Your great Father cares for you, His precious daughter. He who has "summoned the earth" is strong enough to carry any burden. Trust Him and "turn all your anxiety over to God because he cares for you" (1 Peter 5:7).

But I will sing about your strength. In the morning I
will joyfully sing about your mercy. You have been my
stronghold and a place of safety in times of trouble.

Psalm 59:16

Sing a Song

A few decades ago, a Christian couple from Hawaii decided to begin a music ministry. They hit the recording studio and then hit the road, traveling to churches and concert halls across the nation. Aptly named "The Hawaiians," they presented island music with a gospel message. When introducing his wife to the audience, the husband would speak of her amazing ability to sing a clear and strong high C immediately upon waking in the morning.

The thought of singing a high C first thing in the morning might seem laughable to you. You may, in fact, not even know what a high C sounds like! And this might be one of those days when the weight of all your cares is so heavy, well, who would even want to sing?

As God's daughter, you can go to your Father with songs of joy or sorrow. Sing, "Abba," which simply means, "Daddy." The pure music from the heart of a woman of God, whether in jubilation or grief, will be welcomed by Him. As David, the psalmist and a skilled musician in his own right suggested, God will meet your needs with strength and mercy. He will be your stronghold and place of safety during the rough patches.

No matter what your voice sounds like in this world, know that your song is more precious to God's ears than the voices of angels. Sing a song of praise to Him right now.

Lord,

thank You for Your strength that supports me daily and for the mercy You shower upon me. Help me to never lose sight of the circle of Your arms. May my songs of praise be a blessing to You as I respond to Your awesome love for me.

A Heavenly Father,

on the days when I feel
lost and alone, help me
to remember to look for
You. Thank You for Your
promise to be near me.
This morning let me re-
member Your faithfulness
to me, even in my "dry,
parched land."

O God, you are my God. At dawn I search for you.
My soul thirsts for you. My body longs for you in a dry,
parched land where there is no water.
Psalm 63:1

Life's Deserts

Have you ever found yourself feeling that you are in a "dry, parched land where there is no water"? Does it seem like the spark of life has disappeared even from your relationship with God? It's hot and exhausting to be in the desert of the soul—dried up spiritually.

David had done his share of running and hiding in the desert as he was hunted by King Saul. But when David found himself feeling dry and weary, he sought after his heavenly Father and declared, "My soul clings to you. Your right hand supports me" (63:8). David did not wait until he felt fulfilled—he actively sought after and clung to God!

Throughout the Psalms, David's laments are full of sorrow. God felt so far away. Perhaps you know how it feels to search for God as dawn breaks. You have felt the days stretch before you like a desert. It might be a rocky desert, full of specific trials that assail you, or it might be a desert of endless dunes that exhausts you. Either way, you long for the relief of an oasis; you long for comfort from your heavenly Father.

When you are in a desert and God seems far away, follow David's example. Cling to God and say to Him, "You have been my help. In the shadow of your wings, I sing joyfully" (63:7).

May they fear you as long as the sun and moon shine—
throughout every generation.
Psalm 72:5

Sun Sparkles

Sometimes the sky is so bright and clear, the sun so warm and intense, that we almost feel we could reach out and touch its very rays, grabbing them to save in our pocket for a rainy day. Sunbeams have a magical quality. They bring warmth and smiles to the faces of people across all generations—from the youngest child set free to run in the field to the oldest woman sitting in her front porch swing. God's creation truly has a magical quality, and along with the psalmist, we long for people throughout every generation to know God and be in awe of Him.

You have the opportunity to shape the future by teaching the next generation about God. As wise King Solomon suggested in Psalm 72, the fear or reverence of the Lord is a goal to strive for. God draws us to Himself through His truth. The love He has shown you through His Son Jesus Christ will last far longer than your lifetime. Just as the sun will thrive long after your last breath, the gospel will ring true into eternity.

As you begin this day, think about who you could impact today. Is there someone in your life who doesn't know about Jesus? Is there a younger person who needs encouragement? Make today a day of intentional legacy building. Celebrate the sunbeams with someone you love!

Father God,

thank You for giving me lovely reminders of Your presence and creation. I praise You for the beauty of the sun sparkles. Help me to celebrate this beauty with others and to find ways to share my faith with those younger than me.

Father,

I'm amazed that You sing over me with joy. You are more glorious than the most vibrant sunrise, and I praise You for giving me another day to worship You here on earth. Use me to bring joy to another person's life today. Guide me to ways I can bring You glory in my daily activities.

*Satisfy us every morning with your mercy so that we may
sing joyfully and rejoice all our days.*
Psalm 90:14

A Fresh Start

Each new day brings the chance to start your life off fresh. The
sun's rays stretch out their beams of light across the horizon,
reaching higher and higher across the backdrop of the endless blue-
hued atmosphere, reminding you that you, too can stretch out across
your world and make an impact. Your dreams and goals expand with
each faith-filled thought, and your possibilities are ever growing as
you seek the Lord's guidance.

Sometimes your dreams may be simple. Sometimes your goal
may simply be to make it through the day with a smile on your face,
even if your forecast turns to showers. The magnitude of the thought
isn't the focus; your dependence in God is what matters. Today, you
have a brand new chance to live your life closer to the Lord.

What dreams are in your heart today? What thoughts fill your
mind with joy? Dare to dream of a life more abundant than yesterday—a life full of joy and praise to the Father.

Dear friend, the Lord loves you. He sings over you and rejoices
that you are His child. Doesn't that bring a sweet melody of gratitude
to your lips? Sing to Him today. As you start your day, sing a song of
praise to God.

As high as the heavens are above the earth—that is how vast his mercy is toward those who fear him. As far as the east is from the west—that is how far he has removed our rebellious acts from himself.
Psalm 103:11–12

Out of Sight

Think about the marvelous promises within these verses: The mercy God provides is boundless, and He will be faithful to remove your sins from you by an immeasurable distance.

Why is God willing to do such a thing for you? Maybe we need to go back to the Garden of Eden to find out.

God never intended that His creation should suffer. But when Eve gave in to temptation, suffering became a part of His perfect universe. One small act of disobedience resulted in all of humanity needing a Savior who could reconcile them with God. Because of His great mercy, Jesus became the Savior through His sacrifice on the cross, followed by His glorious resurrection.

So what's your part in the equation? If you are born again, then Jesus Christ is your Savior. Therefore, when you commit rebellious acts (sins) and genuinely repent, Jesus removes your sins from you, and from Himself, as far as the east is from the west.

Hard to understand, isn't it? The Creator loves you—and every person—so much He provided a way for you to be blameless, spotless, and pure. No matter how you've disappointed God by what you've thought, done, or left undone, by your act of repentance coupled with His vast mercy, it's all gone!

Gone. Out of sight. Out of mind.

That's something to smile about all day long.

Dear Lord

thank You for Your mercy.
Help me to recognize my
rebellious acts and come
to You in true repentance.
I praise You for providing
for me a way to be blame-
less in God's sight.

Dear Lord,

thank You for providing me with food and drink that keep my physical body healthy. But more importantly, thank You for giving me daily bread and living water which sustain my spirit.

Let them give thanks to the LORD because of his mercy. He performed his miracles for Adam's descendants. He gave plenty to drink to those who were thirsty. He filled those who were hungry with good food.
Psalm 107:8–9

Good Food

If you've ever been on a diet or are a health-conscious woman, you know what constitutes good food: fresh fruits and vegetables, lean meats, low carbs, and as little fat as possible. Candy bars, potato chips, and chocolate (unfortunately!) are considered the enemy.

The Bible mentions food and drink quite often, from the miraculous manna which fell from heaven and fed the Hebrews in the wilderness to Jesus feeding over five thousand people with only a few loaves of bread and some fish.

Yet the most important reference to food is when Jesus proclaims that He is the bread of life (John 6:35) and giver of living water (John 4:10). You might think it strange that Jesus uses such common fare to describe Himself. Yet what is more important to sustain life than bread and water?

You can partake of this amazing sustenance. How? By opening your Bible. Feast upon God's Word. Drink in the message He has for you each day. The psalm writer exclaims that God will give plenty to drink to those who are thirsty and fill the hungry with good food. Feasting in this way will help you develop excellent spiritual health. And the more you devour, the hungrier you'll be for more.

Start each morning with a balanced breakfast, including a healthy helping of God's Word. After all, it's the most important meal of the day!

My heart is confident, O God. I want to sing and make music even with
my soul. Wake up, harp and lyre! I want to wake up at dawn.
Psalm 108:1–2

Share the Music

A popular Christian musician once stated in an interview that he would often wake up with the sunrise as that was the best time to write music. He said there were times when he'd fall asleep with music in his soul and awaken with song lyrics in his mind.

This musician isn't the only person who feels the Savior's music in his soul. Like a tune that turns over and over in your mind, the blessings of God should fill your heart to overflowing. And when the love spills over, there's nothing else to do but share it with those around you.

As a Christian, you are called by God to share His love. Take a moment and think about how you, personally, have done just that. Remember that any simple act of kindness toward others allows God's love to shine through you. You held the door at the mall for the lady with the massive stroller. You smiled and spoke kindly to the waitress who was obviously having a bad day. You didn't lose your temper when a co-worker misplaced important paperwork. You helped your child with his homework.

You might say, "Oh, come on. Doing those things comes naturally!"

Not to everyone. Because you are filled with the love of Jesus, His light shines through you. Be ready for the time when someone asks, "What is it that makes you different?" Trust that He will make your heart confident as you share the music.

Dear Lord,

thank You for filling my soul with the music of Your love. You have filled me to overflowing and I can't keep Your song to myself. Help me to see opportunities to share Your love with friends and strangers alike.

Lord,

I want to be a light in the world. I want to show others how much You mean to me, and how much I love You. I want to keep growing in my faith. Give me a hunger to read Your Word and to know You more.

But the path of righteous people is like the light of dawn
that becomes brighter and brighter until it reaches midday.
Proverbs 4:18

Splendor on the Journey

From a faint glimpse on the horizon to the brilliance of the noonday sun, the rising path of colors and heat shift and shape the sun as it inches above the earth's edge. What begins as the tiniest display becomes a bold proclamation of heat, rays, and light.

Do you remember the day you first heard about God? Your initial brush with the divine has merged with the many days of faith building since, creating a faint light, then a stronger light in the world. You are a witness to those around you, showing others what it means to be a Christian. Think about how much you've already grown in faith since you began your Christian journey. Just as you've come this far, you also have a long adventure ahead—a beautiful and glorious journey with the Lord. The sun rises, peaks at noonday, but has a longer path ahead as it travels toward sunset.

Today, celebrate who you are in Christ. Don't forget, Jesus says you are the light of the world. Take time to dwell on the layers of your faith and how each opportunity for growth is like the colorful layers of the sun's rising and setting. The many layers of who God has created you to be become a beautiful display for the world around you to see. Others will see who you are, what you believe, and how God is using you for His glory.

Your faith is more precious than gold, and by passing the test,
it gives praise, glory, and honor to God.
1 Peter 1:7

Genuine Gold

Since prehistoric times, gold has been known and valued for its splendor and strength. It's mentioned frequently in the Old Testament, starting with Genesis 2:11, and is one of the gifts from the wise men to Jesus. In medieval times, gold was often seen as beneficial for health, reasoning that something that scarce and beautiful had to be healthy. Today, the top prize from the Nobel Prizes to the Olympics are gold medals. Scripture tells us that in heaven the streets are paved with gold (Revelation 21:21).

Gold's yellow color and reflective property make it quite eye-catching. Pure gold withstands heat and is eternal—it does not tarnish or corrode.

Perhaps these qualities are why faith is compared to gold. Your loving heavenly Father wants you to have a pure, strong, and healthy faith in Him. Life's trials and troubles can mature your faith if you let them. And when you have genuine faith, then you are reflective of God.

This morning, remember that your suffering, disappointment, frustration, questioning, or doubt is temporary and, as it passes through this fire of testing, will only become stronger.

Now put on some glittery gold jewelry (even if it isn't real!) and smile that your faith is genuine gold.

Dear Father,

I trust Your pure and powerful love for me. I realize that life will always serve up different kinds of troubles, but they can make my faith stronger. Remind me that You are with me in my problems and help me to be happy in spite of them.

A Father God, help me spend time with You today to see myself more clearly. Please examine my actions, the mirror of my heart, and show me a clear image of myself and how to improve it.

As a face is reflected in water, so a person is
reflected by his heart.
Proverbs 27:19

A Heart Mirror

Toddlers love to look at themselves in mirrors. They giggle and laugh, making faces at their image. Watch them get closer, turn sideways and raise their eyes wide open. They scrutinize their reactions. They probably even give a sloppy kiss to the new friend in the glass—who kisses them right back! What amazing detail their faces portray! What sweet, unblemished joy!

As you get older, mirrors become more of a necessity than a joy. You want to make sure your hair isn't sticking in all directions and that your lipstick is only stuck to your lips and not your teeth. You want to look your best, and the mirror helps you see yourself clearly.

Yet that's only a part of who you are. A mirror doesn't show what you're really like deep on the inside. That, as the verse says, is reflected by your heart.

You probably spend a good amount of time in front of the mirror, but how much time do you spend examining the details of your inner life? What does your heart say about you? Just like a mirror reflects a person's face, so your actions portray your heart. It's good to occasionally sit quietly and examine your expression to the world. What do other people see when they're with you?

Jesus can help you improve your reflection. Simply ask Him for assistance. Ask that His glory will shine through you in all you do.

The day and the night are yours.
You set the moon and the sun in their places.
Psalm 74:16

Diving into Your Day

Some days you awaken, sit on the edge of your bed, and wonder what you'll be diving into today. Maybe it's a pool of busy-ness, or of concern, or of leftover trouble from yesterday. Looking down, you're not sure you're ready to take the dive. After all, it could end up being cool and refreshing—the situation could turn out positive. Or it could end up being a difficult dive with a rather painful "belly flop" to finish it off.

The psalmist proclaims the truth that God owns today, your day, and that His power set the moon and sun in their places. The writer trusted that God would deliver him from his enemies. He cried out to the Lord, asking God to remember him and his people as they were surrounded by trouble. He didn't know what he'd be diving into, but he wanted God there to catch him.

What are you diving into today? Take your stance and don't look down; instead, look up to God. Stand in the bold truth that the Lord has created your day and night, and He will also take care of you in your today and tomorrow. Though you may feel unsure of what the day will bring, God is leading you. He is mighty enough to create the planets and life from nothing, and He is powerful enough to carry you through this situation.

 *Father God,*

I need You today. Before
I do anything else, I want
to know that You are with
me, that You remember
me and how You've
already worked in my life.
I need Your strengthening
power to equip me for
today's trials. Help me as
I make the dive.

I am here

this morning, Lord, offering myself to You so that this moment is as full of You as I pray my last moment on earth will be. I ask this in the name of Your Son, who has promised to empower me to live a life that reflects Your purity, Your beauty, and Your glory.

The one who rules humans with justice rules with the fear of God. He is like the morning light as the sun rises, like a morning without clouds, like the brightness after a rainstorm. The rain makes the grass grow from the earth.

2 Samuel 23:3–4

Last Words

Whether it is a whispered "I love you" or an expression of fear or remorse, a dying person's last words are often weighted with profound meaning to those who are left behind. Last words may capture the essence of the way a person has lived, or they may open a window on what the person is experiencing as he or she is about to inhale eternity for the first time. In some cases, they do both.

This morning's Scripture passage is drawn from King David's final words. He used his last few breaths to reflect on his life's calling as a leader. David communicated the idea that the best, fairest leaders simply mirror the purity of the white-gold light of a sunrise over a cloudless horizon and the sparkling, life-giving growth seen in grass after a gentle rain.

David's last words were far more than leadership instructions, however. His words expressed a sense of childlike awe as David basked in the beauty and character of his Creator and readied to meet Him face to face.

What would your final words be this morning? It is a sobering question, to be sure. Would they be words of hope, as David's were, or of sadness, fear, or regret? Take a few moments this morning to prayerfully contemplate your answer—and purpose to live today in light of your prayer.

The LORD wants you to obey his commands and laws that I'm giving you today for your own good. Remember that the sky, the highest heaven, the earth and everything it contains belong to the LORD your God.
Deuteronomy 10:13–14

He Owns Everything

Imagine you're outdoors. Look up at the infinite cobalt sky above your head. Maybe you see cotton ball clouds slowly float across the great expanse. Pretend you're scanning the landscape. Can you picture a lush, green hillside with speckled, plump cattle leisurely grazing? In the distance, you hear the lowing call from a lone calf searching for its mother.

Now, can you envision a gentle rain? Watch the tiny, iridescent droplets bounce off tree leaves and find their way down to the thirsty earth. As you visualize the glorious world our Lord created, may you be reminded that His greatest and most beloved creation is you. Since you're His most favored creation, He naturally wants only the best for you. His enormous mercy fashioned rules and boundaries so you could walk in His ways, love Him, and serve Him with all your heart and soul.

This verse in Deuteronomy urges obedience in response to a powerful and merciful God. The Israelites needed this reminder, too, as they set out on their journey.

This morning, as you sip on a steaming cup of fragrant tea or savor your mocha latte, remember that the heavens above, the earth beneath, and everything in between belongs to the great Creator— your heavenly Father. Rejoice today that He loves you more than everything else He made.

Dear Father,

You are the maker and owner of everything— including me. You're all-wise, all-powerful, and all-loving. Help me today to appreciate that You desire the best for me. Your guidelines are motivated by love and protection. In return, I want to obey and serve You.

You, manage the heavens and the earth, Lord. Nothing is too minuscule—or mammoth—for You to handle. Thank You for wanting to take on my worries. I leave them now, safe in Your hands. Cultivate in me a clean and ready spirit to do Your will.

Can any of you add an hour to your life by worrying? If you can't do a small thing like that, why worry about other things? Consider how the flowers grow. They never work or spin yarn for clothes. But I say that not even Solomon in all his majesty was dressed like one of these flowers.
Luke 12:25–27

In God's Garden

When spring arrives, many people pull out the gardening gloves and wheelbarrow and begin cleaning the garden of fall and winter leftovers. If you live in a climate that has cold winters, you know the joy of the warm breezes and the thrill of watching colorful crocuses peek up through the last coating of snow. The joy of planting a colorful bed of flowers that will last all summer keeps one motivated to pull weeds and dig dirt. Drop in a seed, add a little sunshine and water, and the beauty grows. In your garden, you've helped in the process, but only God brings the plants to their full glory.

Consider the flowers—they bring such beauty by just being. Perhaps you're carrying a load of worry, woe, or wishes this morning. That load strains your spirit and threatens to keep you from enjoying this day, ministering to others, or living carefree with the Father. Why not lay your spiritual load down before Him now? If He looks after the world's flower gardens, think how much He'll care for you. You're His prized blossom.

Let me hear about your mercy in the morning, because I trust you.
Let me know the way that I should go, because I long for you.
Psalm 143:8

A Fork in the Road

It is easy to get lost in the countryside when you drive off the beaten path. What starts out as a simple trek down a straight road can become more difficult when you find there is a fork in the road. One subtle turn to the left or right and your path changes, while most of the time only one road leads to the desired destination. So, which road is the best one to take? You need to ask someone who knows the way.

God knows exactly what you need, how you feel, and how you make your decisions. Did you know that the Lord knows what you need before you ask Him? David, the king of Israel expressed his trust in God's counsel. God wants you to seek His counsel, even for the most insignificant choices in life. Isn't it incredible to think that God wants to be a part of your smallest decisions?

As you begin your morning, think about the details of your day and the areas of your life that need a fresh glimpse of God's presence. Imagine your options as a fork in the road, and ask the Lord to guide you in the way you should go. If you need God's mercy today, ask Him to lavish His love and mercy on you. Then watch for the ways He answers your prayer.

Merciful God,

You know the areas of my life where Your mercy and grace are most needed. Please guide me in my decisions and choices. Help me to choose the path You have set before me.

Father,

thank You for giving in excess.
Thank You so much for how
You have, over and over again,
abundantly supplied all my
needs. Today, as I welcome
those who come into my
life, help me be responsive
and generous as I offer the
water of Your Word to family,
friends, or others in need.

> *The poor and needy are looking for water, but there is none.*
> *Their tongues are parched with thirst. I, the LORD . . . will make rivers*
> *flow on bare hilltops. I will make springs flow through valleys.*
> *I will turn deserts into lakes. I will turn dry land into springs.*
> *Isaiah 41:17–18*

Abundant Supply

Have you ever been so thirsty that your mouth felt like cotton? Maybe your tongue swelled and it was hard to speak or swallow. With each breath, your lips became more parched. While thirst can be a miserable sensation, God designed it to alert you to your body's daily requirement for water.

In the mountains of Idaho and other states, wildfires often rage on the dry, combustible ground. Firefighters risk their lives fighting the blistering, uncontrollable fires. Helicopters hover dangerously close to the dancing flames, dumping water in hopes of saturating the ground to extinguish the threat. A generous quantity of water is the salvation.

In a message of hope for the soon-to-be-exiled people of Israel, Isaiah used the metaphor of water to explain that God would provide for His people. No longer would they thirst for God's resources.

God also promises to provide for you. And the best part is He is not stingy. He pours out in abundance. You can live in constant supply of God's grace, wisdom, guidance and love—if you ask. Out of His multiplied riches, He generously supplies all your needs.

Praise God for the bountiful things He has done and will do for you. Then, go get a tall, cool glass of water and take a long, satisfying drink.

*I made your rebellious acts disappear like a
thick cloud and your sins like the morning mist.
Come back to me, because I have reclaimed you.*
Isaiah 44:22

Lost and Found

Few things in a child's life are as scary as getting separated from a parent in a public place. When you were young, did the temptation of something interesting ever lure your attention away from following a grown-up? Temporarily enthralled, you lost sight of your parent, so fixed you were on that diversion. But after the luster eventually wore off, you looked up and were horrified to find that your authority, guide, and source of everything was gone.

Sometimes your faith walk may feel like that. You get distracted from the straight path and then one day realize you've lost sight of the One leading your journey. But take heart. The Lord reclaims you. Consider the situation described in Isaiah 44. The people of Israel had strayed from the path. But God promised to reclaim His people.

He continually pursues you. He's there waiting for you to come back to Him when you get off track. It is at that point that God sends your wanderlust scooting away with the wind and your diversions dissipate into thin air.

In the hustle and bustle of your daily life, you can feel His redeeming presence. When things get stressful today, remember His soothing love. He's there with you, reclaiming you, wooing you, His true love. Can you hear Him?

God,

I praise You for counting me worthy to pursue and reclaim as Your own! Thank You for Your un-ending love and steadfast faithfulness. I invite You to be wholly involved in every aspect of my reclaimed life.

Lord Jesus,

I am so dry, so weary. I come to You this morning and remember Your promise to thirsty people, that those who believe in You will have streams of living water will flowing from within (John 7:37–38). Please cause me to bloom today.

The LORD will continually guide you and satisfy you even in sun-baked places. He will strengthen your bones. You will become like a watered garden and like a spring whose water does not stop flowing.

Isaiah 58:11

Dry Places, Dry Times

Death Valley National Park in California is one of the hottest places on earth, and holds the record for the highest temperature ever recorded in the United States (134° Fahrenheit in 1913). It typically receives less than three inches of rain per year.

Even if you haven't experienced Death Valley in person, you have likely experienced periods of drought where you live. Withered crops, brown lawns, and water rationing accompany times when the rainfall is less than usual.

Dry places and times can happen in your spiritual life as well. There are seasons when it may feel as if you're trudging through a lonely, barren landscape rather than experiencing the fruitful life Jesus promised His followers. Perhaps you've tried (and failed) to navigate your way out of this time of drought.

The prophet Isaiah understood both physical and spiritual deserts. He also understood the character of God. Isaiah's words proclaiming God's promise of abundant life echo today across your desert experience. Today God is inviting you to trust Him right where you are, and allow Him to supernaturally guide and nourish you so you will bloom like a beautiful garden in that parched place.

So don't ever worry about tomorrow. After all, tomorrow will worry about itself. Each day has enough trouble of its own.
Matthew 6:34

The God Bag

Our thoughts as we begin the day sometimes set the tone for how the day progresses. At times the day barely gets under way before we begin worrying about its outcome. Are you full of regret for the past or dread for the future? In these verses, Jesus teaches the futility of worry. Yet worry seems to be hardwired into human nature. It is a very difficult habit to break, but it can be done.

The secret of success is to find a practical way to release your fears and worries to the Lord so that you know you really have given Him your problems.

How can you do that? Here's a suggestion. It may seem silly, but it works. Take a paper lunch bag and write My God Bag on it. Next, write on slips of paper anything that has been troubling you: a problem at work, an argument with your spouse, worries over your children, fear of the future. Write each as a prayer to God and ask for His help. Be as specific as you can. Date each slip, sign it, then fold it up and put it in the bag.

The next time you are tempted to worry, you will remember that you have given it to God in a tangible act of faith. You have done all you can—now let it go, and let God work. In His time and in His way, God will take care of you.

A Lord God,

today I will make a "God Bag" to help me remember to give You my fears and worries. Increase my faith and my ability to see You at work in my life today. Thank You for Your promise to take care of me.

Heavenly Father,

thank You for being in me
through Your Holy Spirit.
Thank You that I can set
aside time this morning
to be alone with You and
pray. As we unlock this
day together, I pray that I
will sense Your presence
and guidance.

In the morning, long before sunrise, Jesus went to a place
where he could be alone to pray.
Mark 1:35

Morning Priority

In the pitch black of early morning, Jesus awoke and silently slipped off by Himself. He urgently wanted to seek God, and to find a quiet place without distractions where He could talk and listen.

It's mysterious, isn't it? That Jesus would need to pray to His heavenly Father? In one of His prayers right before His death, we catch a glimpse of the relationship between Father and Son as Jesus was on this earth: "I have given [my followers] the glory that you gave me. I did this so that they are united in the same way we are. I am in them, and you are in me. So they are completely united. In this way the world knows that you have sent me and that you have loved them in the same way you have loved me" (John 17:22–23).

Jesus and the Father were one, yet Jesus needed the constant intimate fellowship of time with the Father. And because Jesus prayed that way, you too are one with your heavenly Father through the Holy Spirit. He is in you.

Like Jesus, you have set aside some quiet time this morning to seek God. You know that today is like a locked door and only your heavenly Father knows what's behind it. You will soon get dressed and step through today's door, so you know how important it is to first sit and talk with the One who knows what this day holds.

Then he got up and ordered the wind and the waves to stop. The wind stopped, and the sea became calm. He asked them, "Where is your faith?"
Luke 8:24–25

Riding Out the Storm

Imagine the scene: a small fishing boat tossed like a bottle in the churning waves. The fishermen fear they will be swamped at any minute. Do you blame them for being afraid? And yet Jesus asks them, "Where is your faith?"

This is probably not the question that the disciples would have expected in the middle of a terrifying storm. But Jesus had a point to prove. It was all about where the disciples were looking: at the waves instead of at Jesus.

Your Father wants you to trust Him in the midst of the tempest, when it seems that the hurricane will sweep your home out to sea and when the gale is about to flood your tiny boat.

When storms begin to test your strength, do not be ashamed of being afraid. Jesus' disciples were afraid, and they had Jesus with them in their boat! Learn from them and take a moment to ask yourself, "Where is my faith?" Have you put your faith in your own abilities or in another person, so that suddenly it seems shaky and on the verge of collapse? Relax! You can ride out the storm. You have Jesus in your boat.

This morning, remember that when storms blow into your life, your Father, who has power over wind and waves, will protect you. Have faith. Your Father is with you in the storm. He will bring calm.

Father,

thank You for being
beside me in every storm.
You have power over
the wind and the waves.
I trust You, I know You
have more than enough
power to take care of me.

Lord Jesus,

quiet my heart to listen
to You. Help me battle
the tyranny of the urgent
this day. May my choices
reflect Your desires.

*The Lord answered her, "Martha, Martha! You worry and fuss about a lot
of things. There's only one thing you need. Mary has made the right choice,
and that one thing will not be taken away from her."*
Luke 10:41–42

The Right Choice

As you read this passage this morning, perhaps you're not
surprised that human nature has changed so little over the
centuries. Most women today can relate to Martha rather than to
Mary. Somehow the urgent still seems to always overshadow the
important. Maybe this morning, by the time you get to this, you've
already done a load of laundry, washed some dishes, vacuumed the
rug, and mopped the floor. Perhaps you have a list of other tasks as
well that seem to require your immediate attention.

Jesus is not saying that these tasks aren't important. They are
necessary for taking care of your family and home. Nevertheless, He's
concerned about your heart. Martha probably thought she made the
right choice. After all, wasn't she hard at work to prepare a meal for
Jesus? But Jesus knew Mary made the better choice. Spending time
with Him was more important than serving Him.

This morning, consider the choices before you. The Bible promises
that everyday necessities such as food, clothes, homes, and chores
will be provided by seeking Jesus first, and spending time with Him
(see Matthew 6:33). Try it this morning and see if your day doesn't
flow more easily and productively.

Arise! Shine! Your light has come,
and the glory of the Lord has dawned.
Isaiah 60:1

A Joyful Command

"Arise! Shine!" What a command! But this is not a command to be perky in the morning even if you don't feel like it. Through His command to Israel, the Lord encourages you to be filled with joy because His presence is in all things.

In Isaiah 60, the God of Israel makes great promises concerning Jerusalem. After His people experienced decades of exile and the city of Jerusalem invaded and destroyed, there would someday be a great homecoming. Many would return to Jerusalem, and every nation would someday flock to the city by land and sea to enrich it. And most wonderful of all, the prophet Isaiah explained, "The Lord will be your everlasting light. Your God will be your glory" (Isaiah 60:19).

Perhaps you're going through a devastating time when the command to "Arise! Shine!" seems impossible to obey. But there is good news: God can bring abundance out of devastation. Joy comes as a result of God's action ("the glory of the Lord has dawned"). This morning, remember the Father's incredible promises for the future. "The glory of the Lord has dawned." He is with you and loves you. "Arise! Shine!"

A *Father,*

thank You for giving light
to my life. I will be joyful
today, mindful of Your
glory and Your blessings.
Help me to be so filled
with Your glory that Your
joy becomes a natural
outpouring every day

O Lord,

I want my life to be a place of worship filled with Your presence, just as You filled the temple that Ezekiel described. You are pure, perfect, holy, and beautiful. I am in awe of You.

I saw the glory of the God of Israel coming from the east.
His voice was like the sound of rushing water, and the earth
was shining because of his glory.
Ezekiel 43:2

At a Loss for Words

Have you ever tried to describe something or someone only to find that you simply can't find the right words, no matter how hard you try? Perhaps you've wished for a bigger vocabulary or the creativity to paint a more vivid word picture as you tried to describe a beautiful patch of sky or a majestic river.

This above Scripture passage finds prophet Ezekiel experiencing the limits of language in a very profound way. The Lord had been showing Ezekiel the beauty of the place of worship He was calling His people Israel to create, right down to the dimensions of this breathtaking temple. But as Ezekiel's vision of the temple came to a conclusion, the limitless God came and filled the temple with His presence. Ezekiel reached for the right words, comparing God's glory to a brilliant sunrise, and the sound of His voice to roaring water.

The very next verse tells us what happened to Ezekiel in his vision of God filling the temple: "This vision was like the one I saw when he came to destroy Jerusalem and like the one I saw by the Chebar River. I immediately bowed down" (43:3). Ezekiel had no words to describe the indescribable God.

Today, the Lord is still filling His temple, you, with His presence. Worship Him for all that He is. And then continue to worship Him, even when you run out of words to describe His beauty and majesty.

> *Let's learn about the LORD. Let's get to know the LORD. He will come to us as sure as the morning comes. He will come to us like the autumn rains and the spring rains that water the ground.*
>
> Hosea 6:3

Below the Surface

Are you a people-watcher? It can be fun to sit and conjecture about the individuals walking by. You might observe, "That man is very well-dressed, but he doesn't carry himself with much confidence." Or, "That girl must be very proud of her body, she's showing so much of it!"

These first-glance superficial speculations are just that—pure speculation. That well-dressed man may have just finished a bad interview. The scantily-clad teen might be seeking attention she's not getting at home. The truth is, it's difficult to learn much at all about people—especially what's in their hearts—based on a surface encounter.

The same is true with God. This verse from Hosea reveals a surface-level attempt at returning to the Lord. The people hoped to manipulate God into giving them His favor. But God was not fooled. A superficial relationship will not reveal His heart. He has a profoundly deep and wonderful bond planned between the two of you, but knowing Him personally is foundational for it to develop.

Has God seemed distant or unreliable lately? Consider whether you have been spending time learning at the feet of the Teacher. Cultivating a cherished rapport with the Master opens the gate for Him to become as dependable as the seasonal rains and sunrise. Tuck that promise away in your own heart this morning as you open it up to mingle with His.

Lord,

show me more and more
of You. Put a desire in my
heart to seek Your ways
with an intensity I've
never had before. Steady
me and guide me as I
dive below the surface
and explore the depths
of You.

Awesome God,

please reveal more of Yourself to me so I can show You more clearly to others. Help me to understand the great and mighty God You are.

O Lord my God, you are very great. . . . You stretch out the heavens as though they were curtains. You lay the beams of your home in the water. You use the clouds for your chariot. You move on the wings of the wind.
Psalm 104:1–3

Wings of the Wind

Imagine the job of describing God on paper. How would you do it? How could you capture the beauty, the mercy, the awesome power and omnipresence of Almighty God in black print on a sheet of white paper?

David tried to do just that. As a prolific psalm writer, he took on the daunting task of describing God in the words of a song. The result is a psalm now numbered 104 in our Bibles. In words that soar across creation, he pictured God clothed with light as with a robe, His home adorned with the heavens as curtains and built with beams set in the vast ocean. He saw God racing across the clouds in a chariot, moving on the wings of the wind.

Exquisite imagery.

As you read the words of this psalm, try to picture the God David describes. Then think about how you would describe God. Who is He to you? A humble Servant, a loving Father, a powerful King? How do you picture Him as you close your eyes to talk with Him? What do you feel when you draw close to Him?

Whatever picture you have of God will be imperfect at best but, like David, you can rejoice in Him, for you know that He is "very great." And that's all you need to be able to join David in singing His praises.

*From where the sun rises to where the sun sets, the name of
the LORD should be praised.*
Psalm 113:3

A World Full of Praise

The entire earth praising the Lord—what a beautiful picture!
Imagine everyone on the planet joining together to praise the
Lord! At times it seems impossible, yet God has already promised that
someday this will be a reality. Paul explained that one day "at the
name of Jesus everyone in heaven, on earth, and in the world below
will kneel and confess that Jesus Christ is Lord to the glory of God the
Father" (Philippians 2:10–11). In Revelation, John records his amazing
vision when he "heard every creature in heaven, on earth, under the
earth, and on the sea. Every creature in those places was singing, 'To
the one who sits on the throne and to the lamb be praise, honor,
glory, and power forever and ever'" (Revelation 5:13).

Praise is the language of heaven. Praise pulls you out from under
any burdens you carry today and focuses your thoughts on God—
the One who "bends down to look at heaven and earth. He lifts the
poor from the dust. He lifts the needy from a garbage heap" (Psalm
113:6–7).

Perfect unity before God is coming! You will be a part of that
incredible time of worship! Begin praising the Father today in anticipation of that wonderful day when all heaven and earth unites to
praise the Lord. Praise Him today for His plans for you. Praise Him for
the blessings He has given you, big and little. And most of all, praise
Him for His own sake, for being the incredible Abba, Father, Lord,
Almighty God that He is!

Father,

You are magnificent! Your creativity fills my world with wonder. Thank You for being You, the strong, just, gentle Father who cares for me. I will remember to praise You today and every day.

Your thoughts

are with me, every single millisecond of each day! Lord, I cannot comprehend this. I am grateful for Your undivided attention and limitless love. You are wonderful!

How precious are your thoughts concerning me, O God! How vast in number they are! If I try to count them, there would be more of them than there are grains of sand. When I wake up, I am still with you.
Psalm 139:17–18

Immeasurable!

We are earth-bound, finite creations, aren't we? Even when we purpose to pursue God with a single focus, we are easily distracted by dozens of daily concerns, tasks, and random thoughts. By very definition, our humanity limits us.

Not so with God. He did not create you then decide to shun you because of your limitations. He is always, always, always thinking of you! When David first sang the words to this morning's worship song, he reached for the most immeasurable image in his experience— an endless beach with countless grains of sand—to describe God's unceasing attention on him. He basked in the reality that the number of God's thoughts for him was incalculable.

This is your reality as well. Thank Him for His undivided attention on you and you alone. And bask in His limitless love for you this morning. He is with you here . . . now . . . and always.

Take a bit of time to interact with this powerful passage of Scripture. Read it aloud a couple of times, then bookmark your place, close this book, and ponder as deeply as you can what God is saying to you through His Word this morning. Thank Him that when you awoke this morning, He was with you. Thank Him for His constant thoughts of you.

A cheerful heart has a continual feast.
Proverbs 15:15

Join the Picnic

Food brings people together. Add a beautiful summer day, a basket filled with scrumptious food, and a checkered table-cloth and you've got yourself a picnic party! Add a few relatives and friends bringing their own homemade specialties, some laughing children taking fingerfuls of the frosting from the yet-to-be-cut cake, and you're in for a regular feast.

A summer picnic is like that, a continual feast stretching well into the evening when the food is gone and the sun begins to set. People linger over that last bit of lemonade and those few final stories yet to be told.

That's what a cheerful heart looks like. Solomon, the wisest king who ever lived, understood that being cheerful allows a person to live as if every day is a picnic. Looking on the bright side of life helps you appreciate the small blessings, the simple things. Cheerfulness does not have to end; it can go on and on, giving you joy for today and tomorrow, joy that fills your life to overflowing. This kind of cheer is a wonderful trait to pass on to the next generation.

Step up to the table and fill your plate to overflowing. Ask the Lord today to give you a cheerful heart. Then enjoy the feast!

Lord,

thank You for the
overabundance of joy
You bring into my life. It
never ends. Help me to
remember that.

Praise You,

Lord, for totally understanding me and for being the God of compassion. I want to be like You. Today, help me be perceptive to Your prompts to show generous compassion. Help me be patient, forgiving, and loving to those in my world today.

His compassion is never limited.
It is new every morning. His faithfulness is great.
Lamentations 3:22–23

New Every Morning

Compassion is a profound, active emotion. It has inspired people through the ages to fund hospitals, mission trips, communities damaged from weather, and programs for needy children. Compassion for the lost inspires missionaries to forsake their own desires and live among those with whom they hope to share the gospel. Compassion shows love and care even in the dark times.

This verse in Lamentations appears at the center of a book filled with tears. Jeremiah lamented the destruction of the city of Jerusalem by foreign invaders, an event that occurred because Israel had turned away from God and destruction came just as God had warned. Yet even through this dark time, Jeremiah knew that God's compassion was not limited by the people's sin and disobedience. They could turn back to God and He would return to them. His faithfulness is great.

Every morning you receive a fresh, unlimited supply of His compassion. Isn't it exciting that you can count on your heavenly Father to be dependably compassionate? This morning is your new opportunity to pass on compassion to your family, friends, neighbors, and, yes, even the unloving or unlovable people in life.

The world will be better today because of God's compassion given to the world through you.

Everyone who drinks this water will become thirsty again.
But those who drink the water that I will give them will
never become thirsty again. In fact, the water I will give them
will become in them a spring that gushes up to eternal life.
John 4:13–14

Fill Your Bucket

The apostle John records a scene of a woman shunned by society, forced to draw her water from the community well during the hottest hours of the day. She carried her bucket in the blazing heat of the day in order to avoid the gossipers, the enemies, and the scoffers. In this famous scene from Scripture, during a typical trip for water the sinful woman found much, much more. She found her Savior.

Jesus shared the hope of salvation with the woman, and gave her a glimpse of what it meant to be a follower of Christ. Even after acknowledging her wrong choices, Jesus revealed the hope of a life with Him. Instead of a simple bucket of murky water from a well, Jesus offered living water—the water of eternal life and the presence of the Holy Spirit. It sustains believers in their toughest moments, bringing refreshment in the driest of days.

Do you need more than a sip of living water today? Is the heat of your past choices burning down like the desert sun? Just like the woman at the well, you too can have confidence that God will be with you—even when you seem to be all alone. Trust in Jesus today, and ask Him to pour out His living water over your life. His water never runs out!

A Lord,

help me to see beyond my circumstances, past choices, and religious responses and see You as the unfailing source of my strength, mercy, and grace. As I begin this day, give me the confidence I need to make it through whatever trials come my way.

$b^2 + c^2$

$f(x, y, z$

E

$+ bx$

H

≈ *Father,*

You have lessons for
me today; help me to
understand them and
hear Your voice as You
give me direction. Thank
You for being the greatest
teacher. I reaffirm my
trust in You this morning.

The Lord may give you troubles and hardships. But your teacher will no longer be hidden from you. You will see your teacher with your own eyes. You will hear a voice behind you saying, "This is the way. Follow it, whether it turns to the right or to the left."

Isaiah 30:20–21

The Good Teacher

It may be that the teacher who did not make school easy for you was, in fact, the teacher who gave you the best guidance. She required that you work hard and, in doing so, taught you discipline and perseverance. It is possible that you were not always fond of her; it would have been more comfortable if she had not asked so much of you. Yet years later, as an adult, you look back and appreciate the hard work she did. It showed that she cared about her subject matter—and about you.

Your Father is the greatest of teachers and He wants nothing less than your complete devotion. He cares about His subject matter—and about you. He wants to grow you into the person He created you to be, and usually that requires some long homework assignments and tough tests. And He can be a tough teacher sometimes as He allows pop quizzes of troubles and hardships to come your way. But He does that because He knows that those will be your best lessons; those will help you grow strong as you learn to trust and love Him through it all. He doesn't leave you alone in the difficult times, however. He is the voice behind you offering guidance to help you pass the test.

This morning, tell the Lord you want to be an exemplary student. Thank Him for caring enough to teach you, guide you, walk with you, and love you.

A new day will dawn on us from above because our God is loving and merciful. He will give light to those who live in the dark and in death's shadow. He will guide us into the way of peace.
Luke 1:78–79

Light the Path

A light shone in the dark forest. The flashlight bobbed up and down along the walking trail as several people followed along behind. Without the light, everyone would have stumbled in the eerie darkness, potentially lost, hurt, and alone. Fortunately, a leader with the bright light guided the group out of the denseness toward safety. As long as the group followed the leader with the light, they stayed safely on the path.

Luke records the story of Zechariah's words as he held his precious son John. The Lord gave Zechariah a prophecy about the future of this promised child. John would become like a brave leader in a dark forest holding out the light that would guide people to safety. He would bring to his people the message that the long-awaited Messiah was coming and the people would find their salvation in Him. Indeed, a new day had dawned.

Do you feel that you're in the dark today, in a time of deep shadow? Does the morning light only barely nudge the darkness from your heart? God can give you light; God can guide you into the way of peace. Ask Him to shine his bright light into the darkness and show you the way through. Then stay right behind Him and follow.

Lord,

please help me to stay
close to You today, for I
need the brightness of
Your light to guide me
through this dark time.

Father God,

show me how to live
with confidence. Reveal
Your truth to me—You
know what I need today.
Help me to see the Bible
as Your living Word for
my life.

*Everything written long ago was written to teach us so
that we would have confidence through the endurance and
encouragement which the Scriptures give us.*
Romans 15:4

A "God Boost"

If you're still sleepy-eyed from a night's sleep that ended far too soon, reach for a "God boost." Grab your Bible and a cup of hot tea, and settle into your most comfy chair. See what the Lord wants to reveal to you through His Word today.

God has given you a wonderful book of promises and encouragement, written centuries ago and inspired by the Holy Spirit, as the apostle Paul explains. Faithful servants of the Lord wrote, studied, and protected the Scriptures throughout the ages, making sure you would have a copy to read today. The Bible is God's living love letter to you. It is alive (see Hebrews 4:12) and packed full of captivating stories and meaningful insight that applies to your daily life. His Word speaks to your generation, even in a world full of cell phones, the Internet, and a vast array of technological distractions.

God's Word gives you confidence to live each day dedicated to Him and the grace to be in loving relationship with His Son, Jesus Christ. The Bible bears witness to who Jesus is and who you are in Him. What better way to begin the day with a heightened sense of who God is, than to read the Scriptures!

We have the mind of Christ.
1 Corinthians 2:16

Access to Abundance

The computer is a marvel of technology. The colossal amount of information available is more than anyone could ever use. Tidbits and data details, history and scientific minutia, trivia beyond imagination or usefulness, world encyclopedias at your fingertips— all thanks to the Internet.

If you think about it long enough, the quantity of information could boggle your mind. But can you imagine how much more detail God has in His mind? More than all the data in this universe, He knows absolutely everything. He knows the number of hairs on the heads of the world's nearly seven billion people, the exact nanosecond of each person's birth, and even the number of molecules in the oceans. Wow! He holds every minute detail about everything.

Amazingly, you have access to Christ's abundance of knowledge. All you have to do is connect to the source. Log on. Be in touch.

If you are faced with a decision or a difficult problem, you do not have to solve it by yourself. Talk to Jesus about it. He has more information than you have and can help you find answers to any dilemma in life. You have the mind of Christ.

ℒ Jesus,

I offer my difficult problems to You before I try to solve them on my own. I realize that I need Your help and guidance when making decisions. You know so much more than I do.

Lord God,

I want to make wise decisions about where to spend my time and energy so that it honors and pleases You. Help me choose to serve You, and not the world or myself. Make my life count.

People may build on this foundation with gold, silver, precious stones, wood, hay, or straw. The day will make what each one does clearly visible because fire will reveal it. That fire will determine what kind of work each person has done.
1 Corinthians 3:12–13

What's Your Foundation?

A building needs a strong foundation in order to hold the structure together. If the foundation is weak, the building will collapse.

What is the foundation of your life? Where do your values, hopes, dreams, ideas, and inspiration originate? Consider this passage written by the apostle Paul. Here, he is talking about motivation. If Jesus is foundational to your life, then He is present with you. This affects everything you do. All your effort and energy will pass the test of time because He guides you to make choices consistent with His principles. But it is your choice to make—either to live by His rules or by your own ideas.

At the end of life, will you wish for a nicer house, more fashionable clothes, and a fancier car? Or will you be happy knowing you have cultivated relationships with family and friends, and that you tried in your own way to spread God's love wherever you went?

As is the case with tempering gold, some works will burn up in the fires of testing and blow away, leaving nothing of substance behind in which to add to a spiritual foundation. But those who choose to spend their time wisely will leave a legacy of changed hearts and lives by sharing Jesus.

How will you add to the foundation of life? The choice is yours.

So, then, brothers and sisters, don't let anyone move you off the foundation of your faith. Always excel in the work you do for the Lord. You know that the hard work you do for the Lord is not pointless.

1 Corinthians 15:58

Stay Put

Wanting to encourage the Corinthian believers, Paul reminded them to excel in their efforts. Apparently, it was just as easy in Paul's day to put forth the bare minimum effort needed. But Christians are called to a higher standard of excellence.

What would this look like today? Although the circumstances of life are different from Paul's time, the two basic principles remain the same. First, excel in whatever work you do for the Lord today. It's not as complicated as it may sound. One way is to think back to the two commands of Jesus in Matthew 22:37–40: Love God and love your neighbor. Is your work today for love of God or the good of another? Excellence means doing the loving thing.

Second, ask yourself what is the next right thing to do? This is a question to take to the Lord for His input. The world constantly tries to press its values on you, to sway you to thoughts of materialism, self-importance, greed, or pride. Remember that excellence means doing the next right thing and not buying into wrong values. It takes a conscious choice to keep Jesus' commands uppermost in mind and to stay put with Him. This choice must be made fresh each morning. Like a puppy learning to obey his owner, you can read God's Word and find out exactly how He wants you to love Him and love others.

It really is that simple.

Lord Jesus,

this morning I recommit to You and Your way of life, which is so different from the world's ways. I choose to believe that my work for You is not pointless.

Lord,

thank You for this
promise that I can reflect
Your glory. Change me,
Lord. Help me choose to
be kind every chance I get
today, and cause a ripple
effect.

> *As all of us reflect the Lord's glory with faces that are not covered with veils, we are being changed into his image with ever-increasing glory. This comes from the Lord, who is the Spirit.*
>
> 2 Corinthians 3:18

The Ripple Effect

When someone smiles at you, you can't help smiling back. Perhaps that smile spurs you to smile at someone else. That's the ripple effect. Like the ripples in a pond, which start out small and slowly spread over the whole surface, one kind act is all it takes.

So, how do you do this? By faith.

First, trust that God's Spirit is inside you at this very moment, changing you into God's image and making you look and act differently. Second, listen carefully. The Spirit is just waiting for a chance to inspire you. Can you hear even the subtlest whisper? Be still, quiet and receptive. You might also read all of 2 Corinthians 3. How do Jesus' ways compare to or differ from the ways you normally behave? Can you think of several simple ways to love people you will see today?

You reflect the Spirit of God simply by the love you show to others. Your kindness will yield kindness. And, like a pebble tossed into a pond yields ripples, kindness flows outward from just one simple act, inspiring others.

Turn to the Lord today and ask to be changed. Pay attention and, when you feel a nudge, act on it. Trust that it will set off many more ripples of kindness, blessing many.

> *That problem, Satan's messenger, torments me to keep me*
> *from being conceited. I begged the Lord three times to take it*
> *away from me. But he told me: "My kindness is all you need.*
> *My power is strongest when you are weak."*
>
> 2 Corinthians 12:7–9

Life's Thorns

As you awake this morning and start your day, is there something worrying you and stealing away your peace? The apostle Paul daily faced a problem that he called "Satan's messenger" (some translations use the word "thorn").

This was a problem that Paul wanted to be rid of, something that continually bothered him. Though it's not known for sure what this problem was, what is known is that Paul badly wanted relief. Three times he asked God to remove it. But God didn't. God chose to answer his prayer in another, better way. Paul was given something much more important. He learned the gift of acceptance, and discovered that in his acceptance lay Christ's strength and peace.

Today, instead of letting this problem prick you like a thorn, why not try a new way of handling it? Try accepting it. Decide to take what life gives, at this moment, whatever it is. Your thorn doesn't have to deflate you. This is the key to God being able to work His strength into you. At that moment of acceptance, you will begin to feel God's power to deal with the situation. Trust that God will show you, like Paul, a different way to look at the problem. Turn your weakness over to God, again and again if necessary. His strength is available when you stop resisting, and start accepting.

Lord God,

help me accept my thorns today instead of fighting them or allowing them to sap my energy. Whenever I try to manipulate things, remind me to let go and let You handle things. I pray for Your strength in my weak places.

Thanks to You,

Lord, I can be wise to Satan's attacks and stand against them. I'm grateful the battle is Yours, Lord!

*Put on all the armor that God supplies. In this way you can
take a stand against the devil's strategies.*
Ephesians 6:11

Shining Armor

Imagine a skier whooshing down the slopes with no coat,
gloves, or ski boots. She would suffer weather damage. What if
your friend was a police officer or a soldier, but refused to wear a
bulletproof vest while rushing to stop an armed robber or an enemy
attack? You'd probably think she was foolish and asking to get hurt.
After all, injuries can occur when people aren't completely protected
against the outdoor elements or on the job.

The same is true for the Christian. The devil is a powerful, conniv-
ing enemy who constantly battles against believers. Thankfully God
supplies protection: spiritual armor. This includes God's truth and
approval, the Gospel message and a believer's willingness to spread
it, faith, the helmet of salvation and the sword of the Spirit—God's
Word (Ephesians 6:13–17). The apostle Paul also suggested prayer
as an important part of your battle strategy. With His armor, you can
stand up to your soul's adversary.

Some Christians go through life's battles partially clad with protective gear and needlessly suffer war wounds. Are you fully protected?
It's never too late to admit you need help to stand against your
enemy. Ask for that help and put on your full armor.

*We ask this so that you will live the kind of lives that prove you belong to
the Lord. Then you will want to please him in every way as you grow in
producing every kind of good work by this knowledge about God.*

Colossians 1:10

Imitating the Father

Is there someone who you deeply admire and try to emulate because you want to please her? Perhaps that person is an older sister you looked up to all throughout your childhood or your mother. What did you do to be like her? Did you dress like her or talk like her? Did you read the books she loved or listen to her music? When you care about someone, you study that person and come to know her well. You try to please her by acting like her or doing things for her. And it is one of your proudest moments to be told you are just like her.

In Colossians, Paul explains that his desire for the Colossians was that they would study God and use their deepening knowledge of Him to emulate Him and please Him with "every kind of good work." God does not require good works for the sake of salvation; the good works are the natural outcome of a close relationship with Him. They are the aspects of a life that "prove you belong to the Lord."

Seek to imitate the Lord more fervently than you've ever tried to imitate the person you admire. The day you hear the words "Good job!" (Matthew 25:21), will be your proudest day. You will know you have learned to be like the Father.

Father,

I want to be like You. I want my actions to be evidence of Your presence in my life. Thank You giving me strength and the wisdom to learn to be like You.

Lord,

I have faith that everything You say in Your Word is true. I have faith that You are who You say, and I look forward to the day when my faith will be made sight. Thank You for loving me and saving me.

Faith assures us of things we expect and convinces us of the existence of things
we cannot see. . . . No one can please God without faith. Whoever goes to
God must believe that God exists and that he rewards those who seek him.
Hebrews 11:1, 6

Real Faith

Hebrews 11 is often referred to as the faith chapter. Seventeen individuals, the prophets as a group, and an entire nation are praised and remembered for their faith in God. Others are mentioned not by name but by what they endured as a result of their faith.

What is faith, really? Of course you have faith that when you retire for the night you will awaken the next morning. You have faith that your car will get you to work, your kids will take care of you when you're old, and the rental place will always have a movie you want to see.

But where does that get you? Are any of those things actually worth real faith? Isn't there a good chance that none of them will come to pass?

Real faith is knowing with every fiber of your being that what you hope for will actually happen. Even though you can't see it, you are certain of its existence. It is like a life jacket or life preserver that keeps you from sinking when the seas of life are at their roughest.

The people in Hebrews 11 had real faith in God. They believed in God's existence and sought to gain a deeper understanding of Him. Their faith pleased God and He rewarded each one—some while still alive, and every one of them when they reached heaven.

Your faith in God is the only thing from this life that will go with you into eternity.

Since we are surrounded by so many examples of faith, we must
get rid of everything that slows us down, especially sin
that distracts us. We must run the race that lies ahead of us and
never give up. We must focus on Jesus, the source and goal of our faith.
Hebrews 12:1–2

Racing to the Finish

The race stretches out before the runners, who stretch, jog in place, and talk to their companions. They have trained for this race, putting in long miles, lifting weights, visualizing the start, reviewing the course, and thinking about the joy of finishing. Persevering through the rainy days, the hot days, the snowy and cold days, the windy days, these athletes have not given up in pursuit of the finish line. Many have trained with friends, to spur them forward and help them focus on their ultimate goal: finishing the race.

The race to the finish begins long before the starting line. It began the day the individual decided to race. The training was part of the race, but everything culminates at the finish. All of their hard work, dedication, and planning is brought to completion with the crossing of the finish line.

Your spiritual journey is also a race with one ultimate goal: reaching the throne of God, with Jesus, your Lord and Savior, sitting next to Him. The apostle Paul urges you to be dedicated to reaching the goal, ignoring the pain and suffering of the race, throwing off the extra baggage of sin. Train diligently, acknowledging that your decision to train is the very start of the race. And keep in mind the "source and goal" of this race: Jesus.

This week, what will you do to be diligent about training?

Jesus,

You are the reason I've chosen to run this race toward heaven. You are my ultimate example. Help me to train and run diligently, throwing off sin and focusing on the goal.

Lord,

I know You are always with me. Help me to cling to You when my faith is tested. Give me Your strength when troubles come my way.

My brothers and sisters, be very happy when you are tested in different ways.
You know that such testing of your faith produces endurance. Endure until
your testing is over. Then you will be mature and complete.
James 1:2–4

Strength to Endure

Bristlecone pine trees, found mainly in California, are the oldest trees on earth. In fact, there is one tree in particular, Methuselah, named after the oldest man in the Bible. Scientists bored a small hole in its trunk to count the rings and found the tree to be over 4,700 years old.

In looking at the rings, scientists were also able to discover in what years droughts occurred, when there was ample rainfall, and when swarms of insect pests caused damage. The tree had been through quite a bit in its life span of almost five millennia. Yet it endured and continued to grow in both drought and plenty.

While the apostle James might not have known about bristlecone pines, he knew quite a bit about living the Christian life. In his letter to fellow Christians, he reminds us that troublesome times can lead to growth.

Endurance makes you stronger. When your faith is tested, you'll find out exactly where your strength originates. And once you figure out that Jesus provides every ounce of strength you'll ever need, Christian maturity is developed. You'll never stop learning and growing, but you'll no longer need reassurance that Jesus is with you—you just know it for certain.

So look at those times of drought and pestilence as a chance to learn and grow deeper in your walk with Jesus. Find joy as you grow.

So place yourselves under God's authority. Resist the devil,
and he will run away from you. Come close to God, and he
will come close to you.

James 4:7–8

Tit for Tat

Quid pro quo. It's a Latin phrase meaning an equal exchange or "tit for tat." You often hear implied quid pro quo. "When you empty the dishwasher, I will drive you to the mall to get some shoes," is something a parent might say to her teenager. When you're at church and a woman comes to you saying, "I want to give you a big hug," there's an inner reciprocal urge and quickly you both embrace.

To the Christian, this Latin phrase suggests that when you come closer to God, He will move equally closer to you. Of course, you can never out-give our wise, powerful God, but this verse shows that everyone has an obligation in the maintenance of this holy relationship. God will not force Himself upon you; it can't be a one-sided connection. You must show desire and initiative. As you draw close to God, you become a magnet that attracts God.

A mother loves to hold and snuggle her precious child. No mom would have her daughter come with those outstretched arms pleading, "Hold me," and then snub her. As God's little girl, when you come to Him you get open arms . . . every time. Some days, you may even feel like crawling up in His lap and staying. Isn't it comforting to be in His magnificent presence and authority? And when you're in God's lap, the devil will run away from you.

Lord,

I choose to snuggle up to You this morning through prayer, praise, and Bible reading. I know, Lord, that You will surround me with Your presence when I'm under Your authority and close to You. This day I will concentrate on You and Your comforting quid pro quo promise.

Father,

I praise You for your age-
less and enduring Word.
Train my eyes to seek
the light in the darkness
and to discern the secret
riches You have hidden
for me there. Jesus,
Morning Star, rise up this
morning in my heart.

*So we regard the words of the prophets as confirmed beyond all doubt. You're
doing well by paying attention to their words. Continue to pay attention as
you would to a light that shines in a dark place as you wait for day to come
and the morning star to rise in your hearts.*

2 Peter 1:19

Beacon of Light

Have you ever been at a low point in your life and found yourself wallowing in a dark, hopeless place? Perhaps in the mire
you cried out for God to lift you out of it. Maybe it happened instantly
or it took months. Maybe words of comfort were whispered to you
by the Holy Spirit, or you heard them from a friend, or gleaned them
from a Bible verse. Whatever the source, this word of encouragement
and hope pierced the dark and shed a ray of light in your heart.

As the apostle Peter explains, God's prophets foretold the blessed
arrival of the Word made flesh, imparting hope to God's people in the
dark and sometimes hopeless days of old. But their words are also
directed toward modern, twenty-first century you, as a reminder that
Jesus' light will shine brightly again in your heart. Isaiah 45:3 promises,
"I will give you treasures from dark places and hidden stockpiles.
Then you will know that I, the LORD God of Israel, have called you by
name." Be encouraged! Even in hardest and darkest of times, there are
treasures just waiting to be revealed to you, who are cherished and
called by name.

Place the words of the prophets into your modern context and
you'll find they are indeed a timeless beacon of truth designed long
ago, which pave the way for the morning star to rise in and lift your
heart.

Then your light will break through like the dawn, and you
will heal quickly. Your righteousness will go ahead of you,
and the glory of the LORD will guard you from behind.

Isaiah 58:8

Misty Morning

In the northern portions of the United States, usually during the spring and fall, many early mornings are dark and gray, shrouded in dense fog. Folks who live in those regions know that in only a matter of hours the mist will burn off, allowing the sun to break through.

Knowing that the sun is coming certainly brings joy. But in the midst of the cold, damp fog, where you can't see ten feet in front of you, you might wonder if the sun will shine at all. Sometimes the fog isn't outside, but inside. Things just aren't going well and it's hard to see—even harder to believe—that the sun will ever warm you again.

Isaiah knew what it was like to wonder when the sun would shine again. The people to whom he prophesied were not obeying the Lord and something akin to darkness and fog shrouded the nation. The people needed to return to the Lord and follow Him. If they would do so, His light would break through and bring healing.

If you're in a fog today, desperately waiting for the mist to lift and the sun to break through, take God's hand and talk to Him. Ask Him to show you anything in your life that needs His light to shine in, to heal, to cleanse. When you do that, the mist will clear and the "light will break through like the dawn."

Dear Lord,

help me to seek Your
guidance when my way is
shrouded in fog. I know
You will walk with me
and protect me. And even
when the sun is shining,
help me to recognize the
need for Your leading
then as well. Thank You
for loving me so much.

Dear Lord, help me to be faithful to You in everything. Help me not to fear but to rest in Your protective arms. May I always stand up for You, no matter how difficult it may seem. Thank You for Your faithfulness to me.

When Daniel learned that the document had been signed, he went to his house. . . . Three times each day he got down on his knees and prayed to his God. He had always praised God this way.

Daniel 6:10

Every Day without Fail

What do you do every day without fail? Chances are you at least brush your teeth and put on some makeup. Maybe you also have to walk the dog or hit the gym for your daily exercise.

What about prayer? Do you do that every day, without fail?

Daniel did. He prayed three times a day; in fact, the verse says "He had always praised God this way." But it wasn't an easy situation. Daniel was in Babylon, the land where he had been taken captive when the Babylonians destroyed his nation. He had risen to a position of trust and power with the king. But at one point, the Babylonian king issued an edict that for thirty days, everyone in the kingdom must pray only to him.

When this occurred, what did Daniel do? He went to his room, opened the windows, "got down on his knees and prayed to his God." Not to the king. Darius was just a man. Why pray to someone who couldn't read his thoughts, know his heart, or answer his prayers? Why desert the God who had seen him through so much in his life just to save his job for the next thirty days?

Daniel's unwavering faith provides an example of how you should never lose hope, even in the worst of circumstances. God will reward your faithfulness to Him.

So, along with the rest of your daily routine this morning, take a moment to pray.

The righteous Lord is in that city. He does no wrong. He brings his judgment to light every morning. He does not fail.
Zephaniah 3:5

The Morning News

Sometimes it can be difficult to set foot into a new day. The world can be a difficult, wearying place (just read the morning paper) and we wonder what difference our little steps of obedience can possibly make.

Zephaniah was a prophet to Judah (the southern kingdom of Israel) shortly before its destruction. He tried to call the people back to God for they had become complacent, refusing correction, caring for no one (3:1–4). King Josiah was willing to follow the prophet's direction and instituted reforms in an attempt to bring the people back to God. Unfortunately, most of the people continued in their sinful ways.

Yet verse 5 brings a ray of hope: Even though the city was filled with sin, "the righteous Lord is in that city." His holiness was not affected by His surroundings. And He consistently brought justice. No matter how things looked in the world, God Himself will never fail.

The world today is no different from Zephaniah's world. Sin still exists, pain occurs, people are hurting. God is no different either. He is still holy. His justice is still a beacon of light. He will never fail.

So step into your day with the knowledge that you're on the winning side. Your God will never fail. God needs people like you to go out there and do His will in your little corner of the world.

Dear Lord,

thank You for all that You do for me each day. Guide me today. I feel discouraged about the pain in the world, but help me to remember that You bring justice and You will never fail.

Dear Lord,

thank You for bringing me out of the darkness and into the light. Let Your light shine through me so that others may come to know You.

Light exposes the true character of everything because light makes everything easy to see. That's why it says: "Wake up, sleeper! Rise from the dead, and Christ will shine on you."

Ephesians 5:13–14

Light Shine

If you've ever gone camping—really roughing it with a tent in the middle of the woods—you know how dark the night can really be. Every little noise is magnified in the inky blackness, making you wonder what animals are in the woods and how close they are.

In the daylight when you pitched your tent, it seemed to be the perfect spot. The only reason it's scary now is that, when you unzip the tent flap, you can't see a thing!

Physical darkness can be frightening. But even more dreadful is spiritual darkness—the place where evil intentions thrive. Before you gave your heart to Christ, your soul was in spiritual darkness, dead to the goodness of God. When you answered the gentle nudging of the Holy Spirit and received the gift of salvation, your soul "woke up." The light of Christ surrounded you, shining brightly upon the evil that once held you captive, driving it all away.

As a Christian, God's light illuminates your life. Those who are lost will see Christ's light in you and be drawn to it. When others ask you the source of your light, are you always ready "to defend your confidence in God when anyone asks you to explain it" (1 Peter 3:15)? There is no greater joy than telling someone about the gift of salvation and seeing his or her eyes light up with new life.

Ask the Lord to let you help your light shine today.

Is anything too hard for the LORD?
Genesis 18:14

Spiritual Fitness

Why is it that getting into shape takes months of disciplined exercise, but getting out of shape is so incredibly easy? We wake every morning full of resolve that this will be the day, the month, the year that we finally drop those extra pounds or run that 5K race. But life pulls us in dozens of different directions, and often it seems just too plain difficult to keep those well-intended resolutions.

Lots of things in life can be tough, like maintaining muscle mass. Scripture tells us, however, that nothing is too hard for God. In Genesis we read the amazing account of God's promise to Abraham and Sarah that they will have a child in their old age. Now what kind of shape does an elderly woman need to be in for that to happen?

If God could quicken the womb of a woman in her nineties, He can work in your situation today as well. His ability to intervene has nothing to do with how "fit" you appear to be. First Corinthians 1:27 describes how much God delights in using the weak to accomplish His purposes: "God chose what the world considers nonsense to put wise people to shame. God chose what the world considers weak to put what is strong to shame."

Lace up those exercise shoes and head out this morning with a smile on your face.

Nothing is too difficult for God.

❧ Lord,

You know how weak I am. How undisciplined, how fearful of trying again when I have failed so often. Thank You for reminding me that nothing is impossible when You are in it.

Father,

I know there are unex-
amined parts of my life
that I need to turn over
to You. Grant me the
wisdom to search them
out and the strength to
surrender them. Thank
You for molding me into
Your image.

*I encourage you to offer your bodies as living sacrifices, dedicated to God
and pleasing to him. . . . Don't become like the people of this world. Instead,
change the way you think. Then you will always be able to determine what
God really wants—what is good, pleasing, and perfect.*
Romans 12:1–2

Molded Into His Image

The world in which you live shapes you, and often the molding is slow and subtle. The way you think about the world is
affected by your family, your friends, and your co-workers. How often,
however, is it shaped by the words of Christ?

Paul encouraged us to think of ourselves as living sacrifices, dedicated to God and pleasing to Him. We are not to be like the people of
this world but to change the way we think. But how do we do that?

You can begin by thinking about what you think about. Consider
which of your ideas, values, and opinions have been shaped by
the world and which have been truly shaped by the Word of God.
Examine the development of your opinions and you will see the
development of your maturity; then consider any subtle influence
from popular culture. This will show you which ways of thinking need
to be changed in order to conform with Christ's way of thinking and
which should be honed and strengthened to His glory.

Search every part of your life and you may find a rogue thought
that needs to be submitted to the control of the Father. Rejoice that
your Father holds you to a high standard and is pleased to give you
the strength and wisdom to strive to reach it. Ask Him today to mold
and shape you into what He wants you to be.

We are confident that God listens to us if we ask for anything that has his approval. We know that he listens to our requests. So we know that we already have what we ask him for.
1 John 5:14–15

He Hears You

What does it mean that whatever we request "we already have what we ask for"? How can God make such a promise? Often we wonder if He's really going to give us the answer we desire.

The key is found in your relationship with Him. For example, if one of your children asks you if she can play in the street, you say no. She may not understand that because she sees that the street is a perfect location for roller blading. But you know the dangers of playing in the street and wisely tell her no. It's much the same with prayer. While many of your requests make perfect sense to you, God wisely says no at times because He sees the bigger picture.

But what about those prayers that you assume would have God's approval—the healing of a sick person, the salvation of a family member, the protection of a loved one? How do you understand His no in those situations? Again, the key is found in your relationship with Him. Do you trust Him enough to let Him do what He knows is best? Do you realize that, in His great love for you, He will always do what is good even when you can't see it?

The promise to take to heart this morning is that God listens. You "can go confidently to the throne of God's kindness to receive mercy and find kindness" (Hebrews 4:16). God always hears you and He promises to answer.

Dear Lord, thank You for hearing my prayers and requests. May my requests always honor and please You. Help me to trust that You will always do what is best.

Dear God,

I feel overwhelmed by all I need to do today. I can't walk through this day alone. I desperately need Your wisdom and guidance. Help me to trust that You truly have my best interests at heart and that the tests I face come from Your loving hand.

Early the next morning Abraham saddled his donkey. He took with him two
of his servants and his son Isaac. When he had cut the wood for the burnt
offering, he set out for the place that God had told him about.

Genesis 22:3

Taking the First Step

What was your first conscious thought when you woke up this morning? Did you think, "Great! Another day! I can't wait to get up and get going"? Or, did your mind instantly begin to mull over the potential problems that today presents? Maybe you're facing a difficult situation at work, or you have a medical concern that defies diagnosis. Perhaps guests are due to arrive and you don't feel prepared, or there's simply too much to do and too little of you to go around. The bridge you have to cross from the start to the completion of today's tasks looks a mile long.

God gave Abraham a difficult assignment—the hardest in the world. Abraham was to sacrifice his son—the child of promise. This was not the despicable command of a divine despot but rather a tough test administered by a tender Teacher.

How could Abraham bring himself to face the day on which he was to sacrifice his son? We aren't given many details, but knowing what lay ahead that day must have made starting it full of anxiety. Yet Abraham saddled the donkey, cut the wood, and headed into history. But a good outcome awaited.

Do you have any bridges you think are you will be unable to cross today? Just focus on what needs to be done right now. Saddle up, cut the wood, and set out into your day. Take the first step. And trust God to take the rest.

Keep in mind that the LORD your God is the only God. He is a faithful God, who keeps his promise and is merciful to thousands of generations of those who love him and obey his commands.

Deuteronomy 7:9

Family Tree

*H*ave you shinnied up your family tree lately? Establishing kinship with distant ancestors can be a highly complicated process involving historical research and sometimes sophisticated genetic analysis as well. Google the single word "genealogy" on the Internet and you'll come up with over 91 million entries.

It's only natural to wonder about those we've descended from, but time can be devoted more productively to the generations that will follow our own. How can you be sure that you're investing wisely in your human family?

As the people of Israel waited to enter the Promised Land, Moses reminded them of the faithful God who brought them there. He wanted them to invest in a legacy of obedience to the one and only God. He also reminded them of their genealogy as the people of God, for He chose them and promised to always be faithful to them. They had only to consider the past—how God led them out of slavery in Egypt—to see that God kept His promises.

We serve a God who is absolutely faithful to His people and promises to be merciful to "thousands of generations" of those who obey Him. That's why the most important investment you can make in the lives of your descendants is to love God and live by His commands. A spiritual investment now will reap divine dividends in the future. How will you add to that investment today?

❧ *Dear Father,*

You are the one and only true God, and nothing this world can offer compares with the riches of Your love. May I live today in the full knowledge of Your mercy and faithfulness.

Dear God,

I'm thankful when the sun is shining and all feels right with my world. So many days are gloomy, though, inside and out. Thank You for reminding me that Your Word can change my internal weather. Please help me face today with the optimism that comes from knowing You are in control of my life.

Light is sweet, and it is good for one's eyes to see the sun.
Ecclesiastes 11:7

Seeing the Son

It hasn't been clearly identified until recent years, but thousands of people know what it's like to experience the aptly named S.A.D., Seasonal Affective Disorder. This condition that can cause lethargy, mental fatigue, and feelings of depression due to insufficient exposure to natural light. Scientists and physicians have affirmed the importance of sunlight to the human body—a physiological fact that Scripture has acknowledged all along.

While not everyone experiences S.A.D., it's true that most of us feel more cheerful when the sun is shining. Sunlight affects our mood in multiple ways. It not only provides illumination for our daily activities but also essential amounts of Vitamin D.

Exposure to God's Word is also vital to well being. Think of it as "Vitamin D for the soul." When you begin your day with prayer and Scripture reading and take a few moments to meditate on biblical principles, you can be assured that the rest of your day will bear a marked difference. You might awake under a personal dark cloud, but looking into the light of God's Word provides a critical "perspective corrective."

Just as it is "good for one's eyes to see the sun," so also it is good for the soul to see the image of the Son of God in the pages of His Word.

I am confident and unafraid, because the LORD is my strength and my song. He is my Savior. With joy you will draw water from the springs of salvation.

Isaiah 12:2–3

After the Rain

When the sun comes out after a rainstorm, the sunshine seems brighter, doesn't it? And with the sky washed by rain, it never looks bluer. As the sun comes out on the newly washed world, you feel a discernible lift to your spirits. The same is true when a relationship is mended after a stormy time of misunderstandings and other emotional pain. Although dear before, the relationship seems all the more precious.

The Old Testament prophet Isaiah described the relief and joy the nation of Israel would feel once they regained the Lord's favor. After years of disobedience, they would suffer the consequences of their behavior when their enemies conquered them and carried them off into a foreign land. But just as He delivered His people from slavery in Egypt centuries before, God would rescue His people after their time of exile. The sunshine of His love would roll away the clouds of oppression and lift their spirits.

Perhaps today, you're wondering if you'll ever get to the "after" phase of a broken relationship. Perhaps that broken relationship is with God and you wonder if you'll ever again have His favor. If so, let this passage in Isaiah be a reminder of God's willingness to comfort you. He simply waits for you to take the first step toward Him. You can go to Him "confident and unafraid" that He will listen.

O Lord,
when I feel far from You,
give me the courage to
return to You. I'm grateful
that You are my Savior,
my strength, and my
song.

Lord,

help me always to remember that You are there to see me through the dark times. My hope is in You, for You are my strength in the morning, and my Savior in times of trouble.

O Lord, have pity on us. We wait with hope for you. Be our strength in the morning. Yes, be our savior in times of trouble.
Isaiah 33:2

Be Our Strength

If you're a morning person, perhaps you feel especially energized as the morning light peeks through the window, signaling the dawn of a new day. You feel like leaping out of bed as early as possible, ready to sing, right? Not always! Even a morning person has a hard time getting up when a difficult day dawns.

Days like that feel like barbells with extra weights attached. As you progress through the day, it's as if extra weights have been added to each side—weights beyond your capacity to lift cleanly. As a result, you feel as if you'll be crushed beneath the weight.

Is today that kind of day? Consider the words of the prophet Isaiah. Still predicting a time of future turmoil for Israel, Isaiah prophesied their anguish. But they wouldn't simply despair. Instead, they would call upon the Lord—the only one who could lift the weight of their despair.

Like the people of Israel, you're invited to cry out to the Lord. Ask Him to be your strength this morning. Remember: He doesn't just want to be a spotter—the person who watches you lift weights safely. He wants to be the ultimate weight lifter in your life. Give Him the problems that weigh you down, then sit back and watch Him lift them.

> *Don't be afraid, because I am with you. Don't be intimidated; I am your God. I will strengthen you. I will help you. I will support you with my victorious right hand.*
> Isaiah 41:10

Strong Support

Gothic cathedrals overwhelm us with their beauty—the cavernous interior spaces with crypts and stained glass windows and ceilings seemingly miles above still create awe for visitors who silently bow in worship or crane their necks in an attempt to take it all in.

The reason these huge cathedrals can stand with seemingly little support from within is because of projecting masonry structures that support the weight of the roof from the outside. These structures are called "buttresses." On most medieval cathedrals, these were designed as half-arches coming out from the roof to the ground below. These "flying buttresses" played a huge part in allowing the architects of these ancient building to create vast open inner spaces for worship. And the fact that these cathedrals are still standing—many of them surviving through two World Wars—is a testament to the strength of these supports.

The prophet Isaiah mentions a different type of buttress—one for the soul. The Creator of the universe offers the support of His "victorious right hand." With the promise of His support and strength, can't you just feel your soul enlarge? As with the cathedrals, this creates more space within us for worship. Best of all, this support isn't temporary—it's eternal.

In the midst of a tough time? God has you in the palm of His strong right hand. He's willing to trade His strength for your fears.

Heavenly Father,

I'm so grateful for the support You offer. Help me to let go of my worries and lean into You.

Dear God,

You know I've struggled with aspects of growing older. My appearance is changing, and I don't have the energy I used to either. Thank You for re-assuring me that You will continue to support and care for me throughout all my days.

*Even when you're old, I'll take care of you. Even when
your hair turns gray, I'll support you. I made you and will
continue to care for you. I'll support you and save you.*

Isaiah 46:4

Aging Gratefully

Have you ever looked in the mirror first thing in the morning
and wondered at the stranger staring back at you? Where did
those stray gray hairs come from or the little lines radiating from your
eyes? Why is it harder than ever to keep your weight under control?
Even if you're not quite at the gray hair stage, maybe you feel older due
to changes and challenges in your life now.

The months and years revolve so quickly that our external features
show signs of age even while we feel no differently inside than
we did when we were in high school. Nothing in our world seems
constant except for change.

But there is something we can count on, however: the love and
support of our heavenly Father. The years you've clocked on your
personal odometer are incidental to Him. "Even when you're old," He
reassures us in Isaiah, "I'll take care of you."

Do you sometimes fear the aging process? Wondering about the
future can indeed be unnerving. Hear the words of your loving Lord: "I
made you and will continue to care for you." So look in the mirror with
new eyes—His eyes. Then resolve to celebrate this season of your life.

> *Rain and snow come down from the sky. They do not go back again until they water the earth. They make it sprout and grow so that it produces seed for farmers and food for people to eat. My word, which comes from my mouth, is like the rain and snow.*
> Isaiah 55:10–11

Like Rain and Snow

When you awoke this morning, did you find yourself praying, "Lord, I have this to do today and that and the other. Help me accomplish all that I need to do and may my plans succeed."

It's not a bad prayer. Of course you want God to bless and prosper the work you have before you each day.

Think about the words He spoke through the prophet Isaiah, though. "My thoughts are not your thoughts, and my ways are not your ways,' declares the LORD. 'Just as the heavens are higher than the earth, so my ways are higher than your ways, and my thoughts are higher than your thoughts'" (Isaiah 55:8–9).

It's natural to want God to help and to answer your prayers in the ways that you think best. After all, you're only human.

But, you see, that's the point. You're not God. His thoughts are different than yours and His way of working in your world is unique. You do not possess His omniscience or His omnipresence, so how could you possibly know what is best in every situation?

Actually, the best prayer of all is the one in which you ask for your will to come into alignment with His.

Creator God

You made the world and everything in, including me. Forgive me for trying to fit You into my mold of what I think You ought to do in every situation. Help me bring my will into alignment with Yours. Thank You for Your promise that Your word will accomplish all that You intend.

Jesus,

please help me to focus on those things which are true and right and pure. I will start by praising You for Your love and Your mercy in the past.

*Finally, brothers and sisters, keep your thoughts on
whatever is right or deserves praise: things that are true,
honorable, fair, pure, acceptable, or commendable.*

Philippians 4:8

Making Negatives Positives

Back in the day before digital, everyone used cameras that needed little canisters of film. You loaded the camera, advanced the film, pointed, focused, shot the pictures. After you got home, you took the film canister and, gingerly and hopefully, turned it over to the local drugstore. A few days later, you picked up the packet with (hopefully) terrific pictures of your family fun time. Tucked inside the envelope with the pictures were the negatives that were developed from the canister and then changed into "positives"—photos. The negatives could be used to order reprints of favorite pictures.

The apostle Paul describes another way of turning a negative into a positive: "Keep your thoughts on whatever is right." Focusing on the positive takes discipline. Instead of focusing on what you fear God is not doing, consider what you know to be true. For example, God

- is good no matter how bad the circumstances might be (Luke 18:19).
- promises never to leave or forsake you (Hebrews 13:5).
- urges you to "turn all your anxiety over to God because he cares for you" (1 Peter 5:7).

Consider also the "snapshots" of your life—the times when God proved Himself trustworthy. Why not load the camera of your mind's eye with these images as you offer God some praise?

I'm not saying this because I'm in any need. . . . I've learned the secret of how to live when I'm full or when I'm hungry, when I have too much or when I have too little. I can do everything through Christ who strengthens me.

Philippians 4:11–13

The Secret Ingredient

Ever quiz a relative or a friend on a secret ingredient he or she adds to a dish or a sauce that makes it so special? "Come on! Was it allspice? Cardamom? Cinnamon?" More than likely, he or she refused to give up the secret. After all, it is a secret ingredient. But sometimes a relative might allow a few people in on the secret after some gentle arm twisting. Perhaps you've been the recipient of one or two of these secret recipes that are now treasured pieces of your family's legacy.

The apostle Paul knew of a very different "secret ingredient"—one that is the hallmark of a life pleasing to God. Instead of keeping it secret, he wanted to share it with anyone who would listen. Paul's secret? We know it by one word: contentment. Paul knew that money, physical well being, or relationships could not guarantee happiness. Having experienced tremendous hardships in life, among them beatings, shipwrecks, and false imprisonment, he relied on Christ's strength to navigate through these turbulent waters. Paul remained content, thanks to the belief that God was in his corner.

God is in your corner, too. Discover the same secret of contentment for yourself as you live according to God's Word. And that's a secret too good to keep to yourself.

❧ Dear God,

I so much want to learn
to be content in every
situation. If I can learn
that secret, then nothing
can rob me of Your peace
no matter what this day
brings. Please help me to
rely on Christ's strength
today.

Sovereign Lord,

I'm grateful that You
have already gone before
me into this day. Grant
me favor with all those
I speak to today. Let my
actions honor You. I trust
You to be my sun as well
as my shield.

*The LORD God is a sun and shield. The LORD grants favor
and honor. He does not hold back any blessing from those
who live innocently.*
Psalm 84:11

Our Sun and Shield

At times the sun's rays are so strong that our attempts to
block them are useless. We've all been there. We're driving
(seemingly) straight into the sun. We're wearing our sunglasses, strug-
gling to position the car visor just right, but still the glare penetrates.
We squint, shield our eyes, and try to navigate. Yet the sun prevails.

"The LORD God is a sun . . ." God prevails too. He penetrates. The
light of His truth glares.

But, "The LORD God is . . . [also] a shield." He knows when to give
us a reprieve. He protects us from the elements. He sends clouds to
shade us. He orders cool breezes to refresh us. God understands the
difficulty of contending with the sun. He knows when we need to
stop and simply rest in His presence

In a little while, your daily obligations will beckon you. Perhaps
you have children to drive to school or you might be heading off
to housework or the office. None of us know what the next twelve
hours will bring. But God knows every conversation you will have and
every circumstance you will encounter. He will determine if you need
the light of His truth or the strength of His shield to protect you from
the glare of false truth. So pack your sunglasses (just in case) and face
the day with confidence. Because whether the sun is shining or the
clouds are brewing, favor, honor and blessing await you!

After the earthquake there was a fire. But the LORD wasn't in the fire. And after the fire there was a quiet, whispering voice. When Elijah heard it, he wrapped his face in his coat, went out, and stood at the entrance of the cave.
1 Kings 19:12–13

Quiet Whispering Voice

As Elijah fought to uphold God's covenant, he feared for his life, thanks to threats by Queen Jezebel and his urgent need for protection and direction. The voice of the Lord, in its quiet strength, calmed the powerful wrath of the raging storm within Elijah's spirit. God's voice became a beacon for the next step in His faithful servant's journey.

From the moment your feet hit the floor to begin each day anew, storms threaten your spiritual resilience. These storms, whether minor setbacks to the daily agenda or major life-threatening tragedies, can send you into a dizzying search for which way is up. Everyday obstacles upset the normal rhythms that sustain forward momentum, causing your faith to dwindle and leaving you to question your purpose. From sunrise to sunset, the sturdiness of your spiritual foundation is undoubtedly being challenged.

Are you sensing a storm brewing? Amidst the storm clouds of your day, allow God's quiet whispering voice to center your thoughts and actions for every step forward. Stop to find that place of stillness where the peace and grace of the Lord abounds. Know that in the eye of each storm you face today, God is speaking to soothe and strengthen your spirit.

As I go

about the business of my day today, quiet my anxieties, and remind me to listen for Your voice. You are always in my midst, Lord. Help me make the most of this day and whatever joys or trials it brings, knowing that Your boundless grace always envelops me.

Father,

thank You for welcoming
me into Your strong place
of refuge. Please take
control of all my worries.
Help me to accept Your
comfort.

The LORD is my light and my salvation. Who is there to fear?
The LORD is my life's fortress. Who is there to be afraid of?
Psalm 27:1

Welcome

Do not be afraid! Do not worry!

When you were a child, your mom or your dad could fix any problem, kiss any bruise, soothe any fear. Any anxiety you felt disappeared in the light of day and, with a hug from Mom, you went on your merry way. Life was simple.

What happened? Your fears and worries kept pace with your growing responsibilities. Perhaps today, decisions weigh heavily upon you and you long to have some measure of control over the unknown.

Consider King David's abundant confidence in the Lord throughout Psalm 27. If anyone had reason to feel uncertain about life's twists and turns, David did. Remember the trials David faced: His best friend's father tried to kill him, and later his own son, Absalom, rose against him. In spite of all this, David trusted in God's love, mercy, and forgiveness. He boldly proclaims, "The LORD is my light and my salvation. Who is there to fear?" He knew that the light of God's love would guide and protect him.

There is no uncertainty for your Father. He knows what every moment will bring. Do not let the fear of the unknown rule you. Instead, let your heavenly Father banish that fear this morning, just as your own mother or father would have done. Let Him be your place of refuge, allowing you to boldly ask, "Who is there to fear?" You are welcome there.

I will always have hope. I will praise you more and more.
Psalm 71:14

Confident Hope

Hope is waiting expectantly at the airport as passengers disembark. Hope is the gentle touch of a hand in a moment of pain. Hope is the promise of new life in baby's first cry. Hope is sunlight at dawn, smell of fresh rain, spring's first bud. Hope is the gift that gives life to all who receive it.

We are blessed because we can cling to the hope that God has given to us through His Son, Jesus Christ. When it feels so very dark, when it appears that there is no way out, if we pause for just one moment and look, really look, we can see a place where hope resides. Even if it seems very small or very far away, there is a hope beyond our understanding—a hope that is placed there just for us.

Reach out your hand, extend your heart and receive the hope that has been offered to you. Grab hold, cling tight. Draw near to Him, and He will draw near to you. He will uphold you. He will guide you. He will protect you. And He will continue loving you. You are not alone.

You can have complete confidence in the hope He gives. As the apostle Peter wrote, "We have been born into a new life that has a confidence which is alive because Jesus Christ has come back to life. We have been born into a new life which has an inheritance that can't be destroyed or corrupted and can't fade away. That inheritance is kept in heaven for you" (1 Peter 1:3–4).

Heavenly Father,

thank You for Your very
presence in my life.
Thank You for guiding
and protecting me. Thank
You for giving me hope
in which I can have com-
plete confidence.

Dear Lord,
thank You for Your
mercy toward me. Help
me to always recognize
the wonderful mercies
You bestow upon me
each day. Help me to
announce mercy to the
people in my life today.

*It is good to announce your mercy in the morning and your
faithfulness in the evening.*
Psalm 92:2

Morning Announcements

What does your alarm clock announce to you first thing in the morning? Probably not "mercy" (as the verse suggests). It's more like, "Get up! Hurry up! You'll be late! Stop hitting the snooze button!" Announcements with exclamation points all the way.

If your alarm could announce mercy, you might think it would decide to go off when it sensed you starting to awaken. Then it would softly cajole you with your favorite quiet tunes. Nice, huh? But you would rarely get out of bed on time. Alarm clocks gotta do what they gotta do. We need them for just that purpose.

Once out of bed, however, you can open God's Word and listen to His announcements of mercy to you as the writer of Psalm 92 suggests. Another announcement of mercy comes from the stylus of the apostle Paul who wrote, "God is rich in mercy because of his great love for us. We were dead because of our failures, but he made us alive together with Christ" (Ephesians 2:4-5). Now that's an announcement worth getting out of bed for!

This morning, consider God's announcement of mercy toward you. Then ask Him to show you how to announce His mercy to those you meet today.

I got up before dawn, and I cried out for help. My hope is based on your word.
Psalm 119:147

Dawn's Early Light

Have you ever experienced a sleepless night? Maybe you were able to finally fall asleep after tossing and turning for a few hours, only to wake up two hours before the alarm and not be able to fall back to sleep again. So after pounding your pillow, you got up in the darkness and awaited the dawn—knowing that the coming day was going to be very long indeed.

The psalmist was troubled because lawless people were coming to attack him; yet he took courage in knowing that God always keeps His promises. He prayed to the Lord and turned the situation over to Him.

In those early morning hours, you too can cry out to God for help, knowing that your hope is based on His Word. God doesn't want you to be in a constant state of worry. He doesn't want you to be awakening before you've had enough rest simply because the worries are keeping your mind from sleep.

Yet, because God is a gentleman, He is not going to barge in and take over your life without being invited. When you worry, you assume you can control the circumstances and situation. But when you pray and ask for God's intervention, you remind yourself that He is in complete control. And you invite Him not only to work out everything according to His will, but you allow His peace to comfort you and bring the hope you need—for today and every day.

Dear Lord,

worry is my default mode. Give me the strength to turn over all of my worries to You, and fill me with Your hope and peace.

Dear Lord,

help me to release control
of my plans to You. Help
me to be open to Your
will for me, and follow
Your leading. I know I will
succeed when I entrust
my efforts to You.

Entrust your efforts to the Lord, and your plans will succeed.
Proverbs 16:3

Future Vision

Every day you make plans or put forth effort toward something—be it a job, schooling, raising children, doing volunteer work. Effort plus plan equals success (at least that's what we want to believe).

Proverbs indicates that the above equation is true, with one caveat: We are to entrust our efforts to the Lord, and then our plans will succeed.

What's going on in your life—not today, but long range? Beyond today's schedule and activities, what does life look like "out there" in the somewhat distant future? Where do you want to be in a year? five years? ten years? What visions are springing to life in your heart?

Everyone wonders what the future holds. Some seek out blindly to discover the future by trusting in horoscopes and Tarot card readings. How wonderful that you don't need to resort to those dead-end attempts at knowing the future. Instead, you can be in contact this morning with the One who knows exactly where you'll be next year, in five years, in ten years. He's not going to lay it out for you, but He is going to guide you on the steps today that will take you in the direction He wants you to go.

So the dreams you have for the future? Lay them before God today.

His brightness is like the sunlight. Rays of light stream from his hand. That is where his power is hidden.

Habakkuk 3:4

The Sun's Rays

Have you ever felt as if your questions fall on deaf ears? Maybe you wonder why the bad things happening in the world are allowed to happen at all or why so many diseases can't be cured.

The prophet Habakkuk had those same questions. He saw the world around him crumbling under the weight of sin and it broke his heart. In the first chapter of the book named for him, he urgently plies God with question upon question. In the beginning of the second chapter, however, he waits patiently for God's answer. And God doesn't leave him hanging. His answer comes like a ray of sunshine, rolling back the dark cloud of confusion.

As God explains, the wicked will be judged and justice will prevail. Peace might not come as quickly as the prophet desires, but it will come all the same. This short book concludes with a prayer of praise. Habakkuk recognizes the awesome power of God and thanks Him for His promise of strength for the dark days ahead.

This small, obscure book of the Old Testament gives the perfect example of how to conduct your prayer life. Whatever concerns are on your heart, ask God about them. He will hear the questions. Then, quietly wait. God's answer will come. When it does, whether it's what you were hoping or not, praise Him for His faithfulness to you. Thank Him for listening and being willing to work in your life.

Lord,

You know the questions that I have. Please work Your perfect will in each and every situation. Shine the bright rays of Your light into my situation so that I may see clearly Your power at work.

Lord,

I may not be as faithful
in my spiritual life as I
could be, and I would like
to change that. I would
like to cultivate a spiritual
life that thrives because
You are able to nourish
me through it. Help me
today, Lord, to send my
roots into Your river
of life.

Blessed is the person who trusts the LORD. . . . He will be like a tree that is planted by water. It will send its roots down to a stream. It will not be afraid in the heat of summer. Its leaves will turn green. It will not be anxious during droughts. It will not stop producing fruit.

Jeremiah 17:7–8

By the Stream

The source for a healthy tree is in its roots. Healthy roots mean a healthy tree.

Roots are meant to go deep and spread out wide into the soil. Roots are the pathway through which the life-giving water and nutrients reach the tree. If a tree's roots are not healthy then it cannot receive the nourishment it needs to thrive and survive. The tree weakens and may eventually die in times of drought or storms.

Likewise, our spiritual health cannot thrive or even survive without healthy spiritual roots founded in spiritual disciplines. By practicing such disciplines as reading Scripture, prayer, silence and solitude, acts of service, and fasting, we can cultivate our spiritual roots and encourage them to grow deep so that God can nourish us with His living waters. And as He nourishes us, we grow stronger in our spirit. This strength allows us to maintain a healthy faith in times of spiritual drought or in dire circumstances. At times when we would most likely weaken and fall, we can remain strong and even continue to produce spiritual fruit through the strength and nourishment that God has given to us through healthy spiritual roots.

How well cultivated are your spiritual roots? Are you drawing water from the stream of God's Word? The tree planted by the water will survive anything. So can you.

This is what will be done for someone who doesn't doubt but believes what he says will happen: He can say to this mountain, "Be uprooted and thrown into the sea," and it will be done for him. That's why I tell you to have faith that you have already received whatever you pray for, and it will be yours.

Mark 11:22–24

Whatever I Want?

As a child you probably read stories of genies or fairies who promised to grant the wishes of a blessed few because they rubbed magic lamps or were simply in the right place at the right time. Their lives were forever changed by the encounter with this powerful being. Perhaps you envied the fact that they had carte blanche—full authority—to ask for whatever they wanted.

Peter's life was forever changed by an encounter with the most powerful being of all—God. He too was told that he had full authority to ask for whatever he desired. Imagine how startling and perplexing Jesus' announcement might have sounded. The wheels begin to turn in the human brain as we think about how to turn this invitation to our advantage. But note the bottom line that Jesus mentions: "Have faith in God." Faith is the key that moves mountains—faith and the knowledge of God's desires. You see, everything hinges on God. Although He has the power to do the impossible (for example, removing a mountain), everything He does fits neatly within His will. He just wants His people to take courage and ask.

What are the mountains in your life that need removing? A mountain can be any obstacle that stands between you and a goal you have. Are you willing to ask for its removal and also to trust that God will act in a way that's best for you?

Father,

one of the mountains that stands in my way is my belief in Your willingness to grant what I ask in faith. Please remove it and grant me the courage to ask for the impossible.

I don't understand

why my prayers go unnoticed
or why I'm suffering, Lord. But
I believe You are my loving
creator and have a reason.
Help me to be busy obeying
You and doing good to others
today.

Those who suffer because that is God's will for them must entrust
themselves to a faithful creator and continue to do what is good.

1 Peter 4:19

Hang On Tight

What have you been asking God for? How long have you prayed? Are you beginning to wonder when—or if—your prayer will be answered?

Is discouragement or suffering making you wonder, Are my requests hitting a brick wall? Is God apathetic? Is He slow? Is He playing a cruel game of waiting to see how long I can hold on? Be honest; we all have seasons of doubt. God isn't threatened by your qualms. He made you and understands human limitations. Through the ages, the Bible reveals faithful believers who agonized or fumed or waited . . . on God.

It's difficult to always keep a praise attitude, especially when it seems you're just trying to hang on. There's no indication He's helping. You hear platitudes like, "God is working on the other end," or "Have faith. God's timing is always perfect." Deep down, you know that's true, but it still demands sheer grit to trust and to obey and to "continue to do what is good." You may feel like the cat stuck up in the tree, waiting for rescue. You just grip onto the truth that God is faithful—and you hang on for dear life.

And you know what? That's okay. Hold on, friend. Entrust yourself and your needs to your heavenly Father. Preoccupy yourself with doing good. Soon you'll be hoisted back onto solid ground.

Photo Credits

Special Excerpt from the Companion Devotional

120 Devotions to End Your Day

quiet*reflections* of peace

Father,

cover me with a blanket
of peace and security.
Give me enough faith
to trust in You alone for
a restful night's sleep,
knowing that You are in
control of what tomorrow
brings.

*I fall asleep in peace the moment I lie down because you
alone, O Lord, enable me to live securely.*
Psalm 4:8

Blanketed in His Care

We all know people who can fall asleep anytime, any-
place—from the dentist's chair to the back end of a roaring
Harley. But most of us have to ease into slumber, letting the momentum of the day wind down and tumble off our shoulders. Can you
relate?

Sometimes that restful state eludes us, not just for a few minutes
as we settle in, but deep into the night. When we do fall asleep, it is
fitful and strained, not bringing refreshment on the following day.

Whether we are preoccupied with our dwindling bank account,
worried about the results of a blood test, or disturbed by a comment
uttered by the boss, resting is not in the night's equation. But there
is an antidote—a remedy for unrest. It comes in the form of a cozy
blanket that covers us with safety and warms us with peace. Where
do we get it? There is one exclusive source: "You alone, O Lord,
enable me to live securely." Only God is able to drape us with peace
and assurance in the midst of thoughts or circumstances that lead to
sleepless nights. Ask Him and believe what the psalmist knew as you
drift off to peaceful sleep.

At the same time the Spirit also helps us in our weakness, because we don't know how to pray for what we need. But the Spirit intercedes along with our groans that cannot be expressed in words.

Romans 8:26

An Amazing Language

No one understands why dolphins protect humans, but stories of them rescuing humans go back to ancient Greece. Many of the cited cases portray a person swimming in the ocean in harm's way of a shark when dolphins come to the rescue. It leaves you wondering how they communicate the need to help this victim.

Dolphins have an amazing language all their own. It's made up of squeaks, whistles, and clicks. Although we cannot hear nor understand them, they understand each other. Their communication patterns have helped save many humans from danger.

Today, perhaps you've felt as if predators lurked all around. Tonight, you cry out in your weakness not knowing what to say. You know you need to pray, but words won't come. You want to communicate your needs, but you're left speechless. There are no words—just sighs, moans, and whimpers.

Just as the dolphins communicate in a language you cannot understand, so does the Spirit of God. He hears your moans and takes them before the throne of God. Our garbled communication becomes intelligible in His capable hands.

Tonight, know that your moans are heard. Know your groans are turned into words through the Spirit. He intercedes for you, even when you don't know what to pray. It's an amazing language. He's an amazing God.

Father God,

thank You for the gift of
Your Spirit. Thank You for
the way you look after
me. Thank You that You
know what to pray and
have words to express
them when I no longer
have words. You have an
amazing language for
which I have no words.